QUALITY
SERVICE

QUALITY SERVICE

D. Keith Denton

*How America's top companies are competing
in the customer-service revolution
. . . and how you can too.*

Gulf Publishing Company
Book Division
Houston, London, Paris, Zurich, Tokyo

> I am especially thankful for the faith in me that my mother, father, and grandmother have shown.

Quality Service

♦

Denton, D. Keith.
Quality Service / by D. Keith Denton.
p. cm.
Includes index.
ISBN 0-87201-551-3
1. Service industries—United States—Quality control.
2. Customer service—United States. 3. Consumer satisfaction—
United States. I. Title.
HD9981.5.D46   1989   89-11695
658.5'62—dc20   CIP

Contents

Dedication iv

Acknowledgments x

Preface xi

1. Service 1

The Importance of Service Today, 2
Inferior Service, 4
Superior Service, 6
Defining "Qualitivity", 9
Key Points, 12

2. Investing in Customer Satisfaction 14

Monitoring, 15
Employee Training and Motivation, 17
Role of High Standards and Testing, 19
Management Support Groups, 23
Service People, 25
Key Points, 26

3. Focus on the Customer 28

The Numbers Tell the Story, 29
Market-Driven Attitude, 30
Service Oriented, 32
Consumer Research, 33
Appropriate Technology, 35
Key Points, 37

4. Dependability 39

Satisfaction Guaranteed, 40
Personal Knowledge, 41

People, Not Technology, 42
Smart Use of Technology, 43
Operational Management, 44
Customer Feedback, 46
Key Points, 46

5. Responsiveness 48

Know Your Business, 49
Developing a Customer's Perspective, 51
Standards and Implementation, 53
Specialization and Simplicity, 55
Key Points, 57

6. Uniqueness 60

What Do Customers Want?, 61
Conventionality, 62
Assessing Distinctiveness, 65
Defining Uniqueness, 66
Making Yourself Unique, 68
Key Points, 68

7. Assessing Service 70

Customer Surveys, 71
Self-Assessment Surveys, 73
Establishing Performance Criteria, 74
Components of Assessment, 78
Key Points, 80

8. Standards 83

Defining Service, 83
Criteria for Establishing Standards, 85
Establishing Standards, 89
Measuring and Monitoring Performance, 91
Corrective Action and Work Improvements, 92
Key Points, 94

9. Training for Services 96

Training for Potential, 97
Intelligent Philosophy, 98
Intelligent Training, 99
A Perspective on Training, 100
Selection and Orientation, 101
Skill Enhancement, 102

Training the Right Attitude, 103
Key Points, 106

10. Incentives and Rewards 108

Extensive Rewards, 111
Monetary Incentives, 119
Recognition, Awards, and Other Incentives, 121
Key Points, 124

11. Decentralization 126

Projects, Circles, and Teams, 127
Responsible Autonomy, 128
Decentralization Through QWL, 131
Employee Involvement, 133
Communication, 134
Key Points, 136

12. Principles of Quality Service 139

Principle 1: Managerial Vision, 139
Principle 2: Develop a Strategic Niche, 141
Principle 3: Top Management Must Demonstrate Support, 142
Principle 4: Understand Your Business, 143
Principle 5: Apply Operational Fundamentals, 145
Principle 6: Understand, Respect, and Monitor the Customer, 146
Principle 7: Use Appropriate Technology, 148
Principle 8: The Need to Innovate, 149
Principle 9: Hire the Right People, 150
Principle 10: Provide Skill-based Training, 152
Principle 11: Set Standards, Measure Performance, and Act, 152
Principle 12: Establish Incentives, 153
Key Points, 154

Index 156

Acknowledgments

Creating a book such as this is rarely the sole work of one person. This book would not have been possible without the faith and support of family and friends; however, some deserve special recognition. I am appreciative of the time Leonard Nadler spent reviewing and commenting on the manuscript. I also owe a special thanks to Charles Boyd whose reading of the entire manuscript and insights on it made it a better book.

And a very special thanks to the following organizations for their information and assistance.

A & M Pizza, Inc. (Domino's)
American Airlines, Inc.
American Express Company
Byerly's, Inc.
Federal Express
Hallmark Cards, Inc.
Holiday Inn, Inc.
Institute of Industrial Engineers
L.L. Bean, Inc.
Nordstrom
Solid State, Inc.
Southland Distribution Centers
Springfield Remanufacturing Corporation
Pepsi-Cola General Bottlers
Radio Shack
Texas Instruments
Wal-Mart

Preface

A recent article in *Time* Magazine reported on the dismal state of service in America. It has become a "maddeningly rare commodity" notes the article. Thomas Peters, co-author of *In Search of Excellence* states, "In general, service in America stinks."

Almost anyone can tell stories of poor service they received, from grumpy checkout clerks, pushy salespeople, and overpriced rooms to dirty windows, poor directions, and so forth. It does not seem to matter whether it is airline travel agents or government personnel, *right answers* are hard to come by. It often appears that people either do not care or make no effort. Sometimes it seems that in service, as it used to be in manufacturing, the phrases most appropriate seem to be, "Let the customer beware," or "You pay your money and you take your chances."

The article in *Time* emphasizes that if American business is to survive, quality service will be critical. Customers must be satisfied or they will go somewhere else. Businesses that do not provide service will not survive.

Service productivity basically has not increased in more than a decade. This is a drag on our economy. The time has come for us to stop undervaluing service. Nine out of every ten new jobs are in service occupations. Yet, despite all this evidence, business has been relatively slow to react. Today things are changing rapidly.

Quality Service is the result of several years of work and hundreds of hours of interviews with some of America's top service providers. It is the story of American Airlines, Federal Express, and Southland Corporation. It is the story of both large corporations like American Express and small ones like SRC of PBS's "Growing a Business" fame. Most importantly though, it is a story of how to improve quality service in America.

Although there certainly appear to be no perfect "10's" when it comes to quality service, there are many ways a business can improve its service ranking. In this book you will find suggestions and techniques from some of America's best run organizations on how they improved various aspects of service. Others like American Express and Southland Corporation (the 7-11 people) describe how their success in large part has hinged on the ability to focus on the customer's needs. Others share how they were able to get everybody focused in the right direction.

Quality Service describes how many of these companies are able to measure and assess service, a difficult but often essential task. As the old adage goes, "If you can't measure it, you can't improve it."

The book also shows how companies are using a variety of means to invest in customer satisfaction, and what the outcomes have been for them. There are also examples of how successful corporate service providers use attention to detail to improve their profits and customer satisfaction. Some of the things they do include knowing their business exceedingly well and approaching service with an innovative attitude. Other organizations will share with you how to use personal attention to the customer as a powerful tool.

Finally, we look at several ways of improving the dependability and responsiveness of service. The last chapters of the book seek to draw some conclusions as to how business can improve service.

The executives and managers of these quality service corporations, like so many other Americans, believe the American people are disgusted with indifference and the shoddy products and services they have to put up with as customers. This book attempts to show how American service providers are and can become service competitive.

— *D. Keith Denton*

1

Service

A manager of a small retail store, speaking of her employees, noted, "Sometimes people seem to forget who pays the bills." In the case of service that seems all too often to be true. Business today is waking up to the issue of the 1990s: quality service. For the most part, business has been in a "service slumber" that has damaged our economy and our ability to compete.

In December, 1987, *Fortune* magazine reported that consumers are fed up with poor service. It noted that the Yankelovich Monitor, in an annual survey of 2,500 consumers, reported that among service industries only supermarkets rose in perceived quality in recent years. Restaurants, hotels, and department stores stagnated, while the perceived quality of airlines, banks, and cable TV operations actually dropped. The article also noted that the Technical Assistance Research Programs (TARP) Institute of Washington, D.C., which studies complainers, found that the service operations of many companies are fielding over twice as many complaints as they did in the 1970s [1]. There appears to be a rising tide of consumer expectation and discontent.

If you consider customer complaints as a symptom of deeper problems, then the situation is even more serious than it first appears. Complaint-handling in the United States was studied by the White House Office of Consumer Affairs, and some disturbing evidence was uncovered. In the studies they discovered that most dissatisfied customers do not complain. They found that for every complaint at company headquarters the average business has another 26 customers with problems, at least six of which are serious. The cold facts are that anywhere from 65 to 90% of those noncomplainers will not buy from that business again! Furthermore, the business will never know why they lost the customer [2].

It does seem that service is becoming a "maddeningly rare commodity" in America. As a country we are much unhappier with the service we get than

1

with the products we buy. Ron Zemke [3] reported that the Conference Board, a New York based business research group, polled consumers and asked them to rate satisfaction with 19 products and 19 services. The group found that generally consumers were happy with the value and quality of products they bought, excepting used cars, pet food, and children's toys. However, they were not nearly as pleased with the service they received. Only air travel and electricity were thought to provide acceptable value. Health care, hotels, education, legal services, and so forth were thought to be overpriced and under-delivered.

THE IMPORTANCE OF SERVICE TODAY

Historically there have always been some problems between those serving and those being served. For instance, a barbering textbook [4] in the 1950s advised that it was improper to shave a customer with a dull razor even if he was a "squirrel" (crazy or eccentric person). Hostility and resentment should not be part of this relationship but they sometimes are. Customers resent being treated badly and sometimes front-line employees are unhappy with the way they are treated by customers and management.

Today the relationship between service provider and customer seems to have reached an acute condition, and is the source of much debate and publicity. Why now? Why has the quality of service become such an important issue? There are several reasons for this intensified interest. First and foremost, customers, as already seen, are getting more and more critical of the service they receive. Many customers are not only wanting, but expecting, better service. A study released by the American Bankers Association in 1984 reported that more customers are demanding higher quality service. The health care industry's executives noted similar patterns [5].

Based on evidence like this in many fields, management is starting to get the message. In the summer of 1987 the Gallup organization polled senior executives in 613 firms on the expected importance of eight different factors over the next three years. The "winner by a mile" was service quality. It was picked by 48% of the executives, well ahead of productivity and government regulation [1].

There are many reasons, beyond general consumer discontent, why quality service is becoming a more and more important issue in the boardrooms of American corporations. Several of these reasons revolve around basic demographics. We live in a service economy, not an agricultural one, not a manufacturing one. Service already accounts for about 68% of our gross national product and over 70% of all jobs in the United States. Future new growth will be focused even more in the service sector. Of the 12.6 million new jobs created since the end of the recession in 1982, almost 85% have been in the service industries as opposed to goods-producing fields [6].

Demographically, the baby-boom generation is also once again flexing its muscles. This demographic bulge has affected cultural patterns for decades. From rock n'roll to real estate their impact has been significant, and in the future they are likely to have an effect on what is expected in terms of service. Households headed by people between 35 and 50 years old will control 42% of household income by the year 2000. More than half of these households will have incomes of $35,000 and over (in 1985 dollars) [7]. They will be income-rich and time-poor, and we can expect that they will demand convenience and better service.

Another reason for the increased emphasis could be that many service industries with narrow previous markets (e.g., banking, insurance, communication, data processing) are now competing in geographically wider markets. When this is combined with deregulation in banking, communication, and transportation [5], it is easy to see another reason for the focus on service: competition. Since many of the products are essentially the same, the battleground is service. As you will see in this book, it is by service that a business can differentiate itself from competitors. With deregulation, mergers, and acquisitions, there are more and more competitors, some even competing in nontraditional areas (e.g., brokerage companies doing work in areas normally reserved for commercial banks).

All of these factors no doubt have had an impact on the interest in service, but none more than international competition. Recently the congressional Office of Technology Assessment warned of an onslaught of international competition in services that will challenge U.S. domination. For example, they mentioned foreign airlines taking away the market share from U.S. carriers, as seen by JAL and Swiss Air's impact on Pan American [8].

Much of American service business does seem, as one foreign manager noted, ripe for the picking. In addition to airlines, Japanese banking is making significant inroads into American financial markets. Although no country holds exclusive control of quality service, many foreign countries have higher service standards in specific areas. The Europeans are noted for the outstanding service of their railroads and airlines. *Time* Magazine reported, "Americans who visit London typically come away with fond memories of the city's excellent taxicabs and subway system" [6]. If American service continues in the shortsighted "profits first, long-term success later" attitude, it will end up the same as American manufacturing. Foreign competition nearly destroyed many sectors of our manufacturing; its effect on our society may be even more profound considering the sheer size of the service sector.

Quality service makes sense for American business not only competitively, but financially too. Recently the Strategic Planning Institute of Cambridge, Massachusetts, analyzed 2,000 businesses over 13 years. Their research showed that financial performance was tied directly to perceived quality of the company's goods and services. They found from almost any measure, including market share, return on investment, asset turnover, and so on, that those businesses that offer higher quality come out on top. The most powerful tool for shaping perceptions of overall quality is customer service [1]. The best approach seems to have been succinctly described by Joyce C. Hall, founder of Hallmark Cards, Inc. He said, "If a man goes into business with only the idea of making a lot of money, chances are he won't. But if he puts service and quality first, the money will take care of itself."

INFERIOR SERVICE

Examples of poor service abound. How many times have you, with your 3 items, stood behind people with baskets full of groceries because the "12 items or less" line was closed? How many times have you waited an hour or more for the opportunity to talk to a doctor for 5 minutes? Have you gotten a "rain check" on a sold-out item and waited months for that item to come in? One December I got a rain check for an artificial Christmas tree. It arrived in February!

Inferior service is not limited to retail stores. Have you pulled up to the 24-hour banking machine and entered the amount you need, only to see the message "enter smaller amount"? Either you are overdrawn on your account, or more likely, the bank did not load enough money in the automatic teller machine (ATM). You can understand it happening once, but 3 times in 2 weeks? Well, it happened to me. It is doubtful that the bank's reputation or my attitude will ever recover from that experience.

While choosing my son's first car we decided it would be wise to start with a solid, dependable, used car. After several days we found the perfect car. It cost a little more than I wanted to pay, but the salesperson did say it was in "mint condition." I have to admit it was sharp looking. The salesperson said, "I like my cars to sell themselves so just take it for a spin. I think the ride will speak for itself." We took it for a test drive. To be safe, we went down a deserted section of road. About midway through the demonstration (without the salesperson) the accelerator pedal fell off! With a heave and a groan the car quit running and we found ourselves stranded. After about an hour we finally made it back (walking, of course). At the sales lot we never did find our salesperson. Eventually we told them where they could find their car—still in mint condition.

Salespeople who do not know their products are common. On a recent visit to a well-known retail store, I was amazed to discover the difficulty of returning damaged merchandise. I could not get my money back in the department where I was returning the merchandise. Instead, it was necessary to go to another department on a different floor at the far end of the store. Other common complaints include long checkout lines, crowded aisles, prices not marked on merchandise, and not being able to get a gift box in the department where the item was bought.

Other frustrated customers tell of similar irritating experiences. One woman said she felt like a criminal whenever she left the dressing rooms because of the way security personnel treated her. She said she fully expects to be scanned "like they do at the airport" the next time she needs to try on an article of clothing. As we will see with excellent retail stores like Nordstrom, it does not have to be this way.

I could go on and on, but this book is not about inferior service. Rather it is about superior service. We can say that the opinion of many consumers can be summed up by Buck Rodgers, IBM Marketing Vice-President, who said, "If you get satisfactory service in this country from your grocery store, local hardware store or friendly computer company, it's darn near a miracle" [5].

There seem to be as many reasons for poor service as there are stories about it. Many of the front-line service providers lack the basic skills to do their job. They do not know their products thoroughly, or even if they do know something of the product they seem to lack motivation or interest in serving the customer. Customers are simply an inconvenience.

The employee may be the most visible aspect of poor service but the system in which the employees function is the primary culprit. Given the same working conditions, most of us would behave in the same manner.

Often front-line service providers are poorly paid for their effort. Minimum wage, or at least low wages, combined with lack of a career path make the job unrewarding. Service stinks because the jobs stink. Employees cannot take pride in an unrewarding job. Management provides little training and less motivation. If there is training it is more likely to be of a mechanical or technical nature rather than geared to providing customer satisfaction. Management spends more time trying to automate, eliminate, and simplify the technical skills needed rather than developing customer service skills. All of this is often true, but as our quality service providers show, none of it is necessary. In fact, it is decidedly unnecessary.

How many times would service have been improved if the salespeople or front-line employees had the responsibility and authority to make decisions on the spot? Instead we often have red tape, rules and regulations, and a detached, "You'll have to see the manager" attitude. Instead of flexibility and accountability we often have a bureaucratic approach to service. Is it any wonder we cannot get good service? Service providers are not taught to think, react, and communicate.

Such an approach exemplifies the short-term thinking that is getting companies in trouble. Some companies do not even know what quality is, much less how to deliver it. A survey of 307 service firms concluded that most could not clearly define the concept of quality. It was also clear that companies' efforts to improve service quality had not progressed to middle and lower levels of management [5].

SUPERIOR SERVICE

Nordstrom, a Seattle-based retailer on the cutting edge of providing quality service, is an example of what is possible. Tom Peters [9] noted that sales clerks "unfailingly approach shoppers within two minutes" from the time they entered a department. Nordstrom is able to provide quality service because they pay their employees extremely well and have a highly motivated sales force. Later we will look at how they and others are able to achieve this.

There are also reports of doctors and dentists changing their office hours to better fit their patients' schedules. Some hospital emergency admission procedures are changing so that patients are greeted and comforted before they are presented with paperwork. Stephen Koepp, in *Time* Magazine, reports, "In Miami all 5,000 of the city's cab drivers are required to take a three hour course in courtesy called Miami Nice, which reduced the rate of customer complaints by 80%" [6].

Quality service providers simply see and act differently than most organizations. Service is cultural. Inferior service, like superior service, begins at the top. Managers in poor service firms sometimes see their role as making money and little else. They push for quick productivity and want to "hit the ground running." These organizations advertise, promote, and use a variety of discounts and gimmicks to attract the customer's attention, but give little attention to after-the-sale service.

Managers of organizations with poor service often develop tunnel vision. They see only what they do or what their department does, not what everyone else in the company does. They keep books, or process data, or sell, but see little relationship between themselves and customers. Many managers in poor service firms are trained in marketing or finance but know little of what it takes to actually produce a product or provide a service. Our top service providers distinctively oppose this approach. These managers know that often quality products, maintenance, and good housekeeping affect customer satisfaction more than low prices or flashy promotions. Similarly, it is rare for salespeople in superior service firms to say, "I prefer to let the product sell itself." If salespeople say that, they often do so because they don't know the item's strengths, weaknesses, and how it compares to similar products: a dangerous lack of information for the customer and a dangerous sales practice for the business.

Stanley Marcus, Chairman Emeritus of Neiman-Marcus stores, notes, "You're really not in business to make a profit, but you're in business to render a service that is so good people are willing to pay a profit in recognition of what you're doing for them." He half-kiddingly went on to say that the reason there are so many department stores in shopping malls is that most of them do such a bad job selling that there needs to be another store across the street to pick up the lost sales. He performed a little experiment in 1983 when he decided not to spend any money, except for the necessities of life, unless he ran into a salesperson who *sold* him on a product. That year he saved $48,000 [10].

Effective organizations understand their customers and effective managers understand the "nuts and bolts" of running their organization. Ineffective management only talks about quality. Commitment to quality by top management is essential and it takes more than talk; it takes action. In this book we will see how quality service providers prove their commitment to quality.

Management can sometimes fall into an elitest attitude. Sometimes the higher the managerial level, the more removed the manager is from what it takes to deliver good service or even knowing what is important to customers. Organizations that do provide good service find simple and innovative ways of keeping management in touch with customers and the day-to-day operation of the business. As will be seen, quality service is not based on assumptions, it is based on accurately reading the customer's pulse through a wide variety of customer feedback programs. Quality service providers make it easy for the customer to tell them what is right and what is wrong.

Customer report cards are a fact of life for these successful organizations. They encourage customer complaints because they see it as a way to improve customer service. Research has tended to support this viewpoint. In a study by TARP [2] it was found that simply encouraging customers to complain increased the likelihood that those customers will do business with an organization again. By promising to check into the matter, the probability went up to 72%. If the company responded immediately, apologized, and guaranteed to fix the problem, the probability of the customer remaining a customer went up to 95%.

A sales force knows how hard it is to get customers. It is much easier to keep them than to constantly keep trying to draw new ones in. Top managers at top-notch service providers stay in close contact with their customers. They see their services from the customer's eyes. This is true of management at American Express, Domino's, Nordstrom, Wal-Mart, L.L. Bean, and many other successful businesses. Developing a service strategy is easy because their managers know both what they can and cannot do as well as what are (from the customer's perspective) desirable and undesirable customer services.

Because management does not always truly understand its business and customers at the ground level, they often end up making poor investments in equipment, computers, and technology. In many cases, services and manufacturing industries often purchase technology for technology's sake. Computers are not the answer to quality service. Sometimes they can help and sometimes they can damage the quality of service. Surprisingly, many top level service providers do not use state-of-the-art technology; more importantly though, they use state-of-the-art-people management. They know that they cannot use technology to replace people. They know instead that technology should make it easier for people to give quality service and produce quality goods.

Top-level service providers are decidedly people-oriented companies. These organizations recognize that "service is people," not just customers but employees as well. They treat their employees well and the employees return the favor to customers. Employees take pride in their work and pride in themselves. Everybody from the janitor to the president knows how his/her job affects the customer.

How do these companies get everyone involved and focused on the customer? As we will see, there are many ways and they are all important pieces in the same customer service puzzle. Training of course is involved, but it is not necessarily the extent as much as what is taught. Nordstrom, mentioned earlier, has only a day and a half of formal training. It is the day-to-day education through interaction with customers that is more important. If service is to be consistent, then employees need certain service skills. Whether these skills are taught formally or informally is not important. What is important is to show employees what the company is about, how and why they, the employees, are important and what "management support" is available to them.

Top-level service providers encourage, respect, and sometimes even nurture front-line employees as equal partners in delivering services. The organizations want their front-line people to feel good about the company, themselves, and management's relationship with them. When that is accomplished, customer satisfaction tends to take care of itself. We will look at how many of these companies help develop this environment and relationship with their employees and customers.

Effective service providers are involved in on-going thought and preparation. Employees are not just dumped on customers. Problem-solving skills are needed. Authority and responsibility to make decisions need to be established. Programs need to be set up so that employees and management are exposed to the production or operational aspects of a business, then rotated through the company to better develop a consumer perspective. We will look at how some companies use decentralization and job rotation to improve services.

While service begins with top management's support, it ends with the front-line service providers. Top-level service providers focus attention on this level. Employee self-image is important, and so is the need for stress management. Employees need to perceive that there is a chance for personal as well as professional growth.

This "art" side of management must also be complemented by the "science" side to avoid ending up with a country club atmosphere and little production. Standards must be set, performance must be measured and compared to standards, and improvements made.

Salespeople, marketing agents, real estate personnel, insurance representatives, and thousands of other service personnel are an enigma. For most there is no consistent way of measuring their level of service. For instance, it is very difficult to determine what lawyers, physicians, teachers, and other service personnel do, much less how their level of service compares to others. As will be seen in this book, there are some organizations that have done some interesting work establishing criteria to measure service quality and productivity. However, there is little consensus in the U.S. on how to standardize and accurately report the information. We will look at how some service organizations are measuring and improving their productivity and service. Developing and defining such a measurement system will be critical to our understanding of quality in the service sector. It takes organization and control to improve services. It takes incentives to beat the standards and change behavior. Top service providers know the science of service. Approaching it scientifically begins with a definition.

DEFINING QUALITIVITY

Many American businesses have mistakenly attributed different levels of importance to productivity, or how much is produced, and quality, which is the level of excellence of what is produced. Somehow many American businesses saw increasing productivity as more important than producing quality products and services. That has been a mistake. Many European and Japanese companies recognize that quality and productivity are equally crucial. Quality and productivity are two factors in the same equation. Together they equal customer satisfaction and business success.

Many of the highly successful organizations described in these pages have recognized the need to define their business expectations in the context of quality and productivity. American Express, one of our top-service providers, emphasizes the dual nature of a service definition. Several years ago, when they were ready to establish some production standards for turnaround time on credit card applications and other jobs performed, they asked their customers what would be an acceptable performance standard.

They did not look at what they were capable of producing; instead, they asked their customer what they, the customer, expected.

At Federal Express, one manager noted that telephone operators were instructed to meet specific production quotas. There was a lot of emphasis on individual productivity (i.e., the more calls an operator handled within a given time-frame, the more "productive" he or she was). The manager discovered the company was sending mixed signals. On one hand the organization was pushing individual production standards, while on the other hand talking about the importance of quality. It was not working; productivity was not really that great, and customer complaints were increasing. So Federal Express made a change. Instead of having to fulfill individual production quotas, the operators were told to "take care of the customer." The result was that both quality and productivity measures rose. By shifting emphasis from productivity to quality service, Federal Express gained increased customer satisfaction. Employees knew that what was expected was not individual quota fulfillment but service aimed foremost at pleasing the customer.

Jack Stack, C.E.O. of one of our other successful organizations noted that he does not believe in individual "piece-rate" performance standards. He says that it makes people focus on the wrong things; it makes them selfish and greedy. Instead, this C.E.O. develops goals for employees whereby individual performance expectations are based on meeting department, corporate and customer expectations.

Yet another of our top-service providers, Texas Instruments Customer Response Center (CRC), places their emphasis on peer pressure and professional pride rather than on individual performance standards. Solid State, Inc. even has departments downstream consider departments upstream of them to be their customers. The downstream departments' performance standards are thus based on customer expectations of those departments upstream. Everyone from personnel to sales to accounting to production control assesses their own performance in terms of meeting customer expectations.

In their own ways each of these organizations has recognized the risk of too narrowly defining what is expected. They have also given considerable effort to making sure no mixed signals are being sent. They try not to separate or dichotomize production and quality.

Successful service and product companies know that solutions to problems begin with a definition. Solutions are determined in large part by how the problem is defined. If you see business as an individual productivity problem, then it is obvious what solutions you recommend. However, if you see the problem as one of corporate quality-productivity, or *qualitivity*, then appropriate solutions can be developed.

Organizations that epitomize quality service do so because of their focus on qualitivity rather than focusing either on production or quality standards. When effective management is practiced, there is a corresponding improvement in qualitivity, not just in production or quality. If we are to be successful at delivering effective quality service, we must stop thinking of quality and productivity as mutually exclusive terms. Successful companies in the future will find it necessary to define qualitivity in terms of meeting customer expectations as their standard of performance.

Improving quality service will take more than developing adequate definitions of quality and using quantifiable measures. A motivated, knowledgeable, and caring employee is an invaluable asset; one which is needed if service is to be improved. Clearly one theme that runs through these examples of efficient service providers is that people are most important; technology is secondary to quality service. If people cannot provide quality service, machines surely cannot. Listen to these stories of these service providers and you will hear how critical it is to openly communicate, to share, trust, and involve personnel in the service process. As with many examples, top management must initiate it and subordinates must be held accountable and responsible for developing an effective service process. To fully implement quality service it may be necessary to implement some form of supervision similar to those described in this text that, like American Airlines, emphasize consensus decisions and Texas Instruments CRC group's peer pressure. Delegation does not mean abdication of service responsibility. Every manager who has authority over service personnel must have a working knowledge of both what they do and how they do it. It means knowing what is involved. Organizations like Nordstrom and Southland Corporation make a point of encouraging their managers to become intimately familiar with the problems and perspectives of operational personnel. Still others like American Airlines delegate more operational decisions to operational personnel. Regardless of the method the emphasis remains on responsiveness and front-line decision makers that understand their customers' needs and the organization's ability.

If quality service is to become a consistent reality in the United States, it requires that managers as well as employees be judged on quality performance as well as on financial and productivity performance. People at all levels have to do their jobs right and develop a quality interface with customers. This will not happen unless management understands their customers' needs. As will be seen throughout the book, achieving true quality service requires a cultural and perceptual change within the organization. A philosophy of quality service cannot occur unless upper management is serious about making it a top priority. It takes deeds, not talk, to prove to the customer that they are getting what they expect.

Instead of using slick promotions or gimmicks, it is wiser to provide better warranties and better return policies. Rather than hype, businesses need to offer better on-time delivery and lower stock-outs. Providing after-the-sales service guarantees a business long-term success more effectively than cutthroat pricing. Friendly and concerned personnel are a much more valuable resource than high technology. In service it is the people who make the difference. We like those we deal with to know our names, our preferences, attitudes, and needs.

KEY POINTS

If America is to remain competitive American business must find ways of keeping customers satisfied. Unfortunately, service has often been neglected. As already seen, there are indications everywhere that here is a problem that demands solutions. How these service providers do their jobs, how fast and accurately they process paperwork, how successfully they pursue accounts, and how effective they are in taking the extra step to develop customer loyalty will determine an organization's success.

Often it is not a matter of customer loyalty as much as customer hostility. People are fed up. Demographics indicate that people expect better service and products. Despite this, some businesses still ignore the financially prudent policy of delivering high quality service and products before expecting profits.

Poor service has its roots in poor management. Instead of bureaucracy, we need flexibility. Instead of autocratic managers focused only on productivity, we need greater employee involvement, more reliance on peer pressure, and greater emphasis on the broader issues of qualitivity. Front-line employees must have the freedom as well as the authority and responsibility to deal with individual customers.

We need managers who intuitively understand their businesses; who themselves know, and can teach their employees, product and service information. In the final analysis, service is people-oriented. Management must nurture employees; teach them how to, and allow them to solve problems; find ways to measure their efforts; and reward those who serve best.

- Improve management's product knowledge and understanding and support in delivering services
- Improve our understanding of customer needs, desires, and attitudes
- Develop a definition of *qualitivity* at each organization
- Set service standards and improve our measurement of service
- Provide skill-based training and product knowledge to front-line service providers

- Establish incentives and motivation to provide quality service
- Adopt a corporate philosophy of quality service by changing the cultural and perceptional attitudes of the organization

REFERENCES

1. Uttal, Bro, "Corporations That Serve You Best," *Fortune*, Dec. 7, 1987, pp. 98–116.
2. TARP: *Consumer Complaint Handling in America: Summary of Findings and Recommendations*, White House Office of Consumer Affairs, 1980.
3. Zemke, Ron, "Contact! Training Employees to Meet the Public," *Training*, August 1986, pp. 41–45.
4. AMBBA (Associated Master Barbers and Beauticians of America), *The Standard Textbook of Barbering*, 4th ed. Chicago: The Association, 1950.
5. Shetty, Y. K. and Joel E. Ross, "Quality and Its Management in Service Businesses," in *Quest for Quality*, Mehran Sepehri (Ed.) Norcross, G.A.: Industrial Institute of Engineering, 1987, pp. 187–192.
6. Koepp, Stephen, "Pul-eeze! Will Somebody Help Me?" *Time*, February 2, 1987, pp. 48–55.
7. Russell, Cheryl, "Bad Service," *American Demographics*, October 1987, p. 7.
8. Kelly, Robert E., "Poorly Served Employees Serve Customers Just as Poorly," *Wall Street Journal*, October 12, 1987, p. 22.
9. Peters, Tom, "The Store is Where the Action Is," *U.S. News and World Report*, May 12, 1986, p. 58.
10. O'Dell, Kathleen, "Service Sells, Top Retailer Says," *Springfield News Leader*, October 8, 1988, p. 8B.

2

Investing in Customer Satisfaction

Those companies that do focus on customer satisfaction are the ones that have operationally defined qualitivity. In this book we will examine how successful service providers from a variety of fields provide quality service. Some of these top service providers include American Airlines, American Express, Byerly's, Domino's Pizza, Hallmark, L.L. Bean, Nordstrom, SRC, Southland Corporation's distribution, Tandy, and Wal-Mart. In Chapter 12 we will look at some of the principles that all of these quality service providers have in common. In addition to these principles, these organizations have one other thing in common. All of them have a guiding philosophy. They have consciously made the choice to invest in customer satisfaction and make it their corporate goal.

Some of the customer satisfaction techniques are subtle and others are overt. Some involve a commitment in management time while others focus on extensive monitoring of customers' needs and attitudes. We will examine various aspects of customer satisfaction later, but for now we will sample the variety of means available, as well as some possible benefits of, investing in customer satisfaction.

All of the organizations realize that to get any return on investment in customer satisfaction will require commitment not only of management time but also commitment on the part of their front-line personnel. As will be seen here and in later chapters, successful implementation of quality service requires a great deal of thorough preparation and organization.

Customer satisfaction happens when a company focuses on quality service. As demonstrated in the previous chapter, customer satisfaction produces real rewards for the company in the form of customer loyalty and corporate image. Lack of customer satisfaction produces real liabilities and this is a fact that business can ill afford to ignore. As customers, we go back to a business again and again because we know its quality, we know we can

14

depend on the people there, and we know we will get consistent service. Businesses like the upscale grocery store Byerly's know customers do not mind spending money as long as they get what they expect. Demographics and the increase in complaints tend to indicate that more and more people are willing to pay for good service.

While most companies recognize the value of a satisfied customer, only a few have made the commitment necessary to ensure customer satisfaction. Holiday Inn, Inc. invests in customer satisfaction in a direct manner. They have spent over $1 million each year for the past nine years in monitoring their customers' needs. This investment has produced changes in service such as larger rooms, king-sized beds, thicker towels, larger bars of soap, massaging shower heads, and glass tumblers, just to mention a few.

Other top service providers may not make as direct an investment but, nevertheless, do invest heavily in customer satisfaction. Texas Instruments' Customer Response Center (CRC) is the point of contact between Texas Instruments and the general public. They have a toll-free phone number and answer inquiries from their own employees and the general public. If they cannot answer your questions, they will put you in contact with someone who can. They also identify recipients of incoming mail that is not addressed to a specific person or department.

While many 800-number centers are considered "sweat shops," this is not the case with this top-level service provider. Most Texas Instruments employees consider the CRC as a way to improve themselves. In the last 10 years, the turnover rate has been less than seven percent. This occurs despite the fact that they provide the 77,000 Texas Instruments employees and members of the public with information, and answer 210,000 concerns each year. Their goal is to find answers to inquiries within two hours. They meet this goal over 90% of the time.

Today, less than one percent of the CRC callers get "bounced around" or have to wait long for answers. Less than 2% of those who call get a busy signal or are put on hold and hang up. CRC has been able to achieve these results despite having no individual quantitative standards. Most 800-number organizations have standards on within how many minutes or seconds the operators must respond. CRC, instead, focuses on quality standards rather than quantity standards. They want a quality interface, and found that individual standards resulted in their people focusing on numbers instead of on what they were there to do.

MONITORING

The Texas Instruments CRC believes it is important to monitor progress. The center makes what they call a Q.A. (quality assurance) call. They call the customer back to make sure the help he or she needed was received. They found that about 98 % of their callers were satisfied. Surprisingly, they were able to increase customer satisfaction because of the monitoring process itself. Research, as noted in the previous chapter, has tended to support that follow-ups on customer contact can lead to better-satisfied customers. As the CRC manager notes, "We found that some would have gone away unsatisfied if we had not called back. We were able to satisfy the customer merely by making the Q.A. call back."

Other service organizations not only have point-of-contact monitoring but also directly involve the CEO. Demonstrating top management support is a fundamental principle of good service. Wal-Mart is an organization that applies this concept. Wal-Mart discount stores have had unbelievable growth and success in part because of their customer satisfaction and loyalty. Customers like Wal-Mart's prices, selection, and policy of accepting returned merchandise without question. Typically their customers make more trips to their stores than those of their competitors. Studies have shown that customers believed they got more of the merchandise they wanted at lower prices.

Sam Walton, the principle owner, makes a point of maintaining close ties with his stores. He monitors through personal visits. Monday through Friday he and his top executives visit several stores. At one time Sam Walton even knew his stores' personnel on a first name basis. Today, with hundreds of stores, this is impossible, but his philosophy of monitoring and maintaining close ties is carried down through the individual store managers. These managers make a point of being "down on the floor" listening and talking to their department managers and customers. They do listen. In fact, some store managers note that over 73 % of their store merchandise is purchased through department managers working on the sales floor. This is in stark contrast to the centralized ordering and purchasing of most discount stores.

Another highly successful service organization, Southland Corporation (the 7-Eleven people) also expects their managers to monitor customers' satisfaction by maintaining close ties with customers. Each year corporate headquarters staff work in local 7-Eleven stores to get a better perspective on what works and does not work.

As will be seen, while top service providers may use varied techniques, they all want their managers to understand their respective customers better. Some even rotate managers throughout the organization; managers actually work as front-line service personnel so they do not lose the ground-level operational perspective. Other companies find equally innovative ways of exposing their managers to the customers' perspective.

Even as there are many ways to monitor customer satisfaction, it is clear that doing so is critical to maintaining the service that customers want. Monitoring allows companies to offer the quality and merchandise that customers expect, and provide the services that mean something to their customers.

As in the Texas Instruments CRC case and as research supports, a frequent bonus of a monitoring process is that it actually seems to enhance satisfaction. Customers generally appreciate the fact that someone asks for their opinions and appears truly concerned with their responses. Nobody likes to believe a business is only interested in their money. If a business obtains the customer's satisfaction it gets more than money: it obtains the kind of customer loyalty that is the backbone of organizations like Wal-Mart and other successful enterprises.

EMPLOYEE TRAINING AND MOTIVATION

Monitoring the quality of service is important, but alone is not enough to ensure long-term success and customer satisfaction. Service, more so than manufacturing, is people-dependent. Services are not generated by machines, they are produced by people. As Will Rogers once said, "Numbers don't mean nothin'! It's people that count." This certainly holds true for service. Measurement and technology are important, but the key ingredient in good service is people, particularly the point-of-contact people. Texas Instruments CRC manager, Georgia A. Kendrick notes, "People are most important, equipment is secondary." If you have grumpy salespeople or checkers, no amount of technology will help. If employees do not care or are not appreciated, customer and employee loyalty will soon disappear.

Texas Instruments CRC is not the only organization that has extensive training. Most organizations that effectively provide quality service are able to enhance their image of consistent customer service through their ongoing training and motivation programs. Holiday Inn believes so much in training that they have the industry's first training institute for hotel managers.

American Express is seen by many, including *Fortune* magazine, to be the top service provider in its field. Like Texas Instruments' CRC and Holiday Inn, the company puts great faith in employee training. New managers are selected from "high potential" personnel recommended by their superiors. These people, who already have five to six years experience, then join the corporate headquarters staff for one or two years. At corporate headquarters they receive in-depth training. Then the new manager usually returns to his/her local environment to become head of a particular area: operations, finance, sales, and so on.

Of course every organization provides some training; it's just that some are more serious about it. Very few companies invest in as much training and communication as Springfield Remanufacturing Corporation (SRC). The company is one of the best run small businesses in the United States.

They have been featured in *INC.* magazine, and were the focus of a PBS special called "Growing a Business." SRC rebuilds or recycles engines and engine components. They have had a phenomenal sales growth rate, averaging 25% through 1988. Much of this growth has been attributed to customer satisfaction. At a one percent warranty rate compared to an industry average of four percent, SRC has the highest quality and lowest return rate in the industry.

What is special about this organization is the air of openness and trust between labor and management. Jack Stack, president of the company, notes, "There's not a financial number that our employees don't know about or have access to!" Motivational efforts are straightforward. Weekly meetings are conducted with all personnel to review financial information so employees can see the relationship between their jobs and the profit and success of the company.

Wal-Mart also makes a policy of openly sharing financial information, although they do not provide as intensive training in financial matters as SRC does. One Wal-Mart store manager, Ralph Graham, mentioned, "We share our store sales, profits, losses, purchase mark-ups, rate of inventory, turnover, and so on." This process of sharing information not only seems to build up trust between members of the organization but also helps customer satisfaction, since employees can see the results of their interactions with the public.

We can note that SRC's training program goes beyond merely training in the financial aspects of a business. They train at all levels, ranging from key executive positions, engineers, and accountants, to their hourly-paid personnel. However, it is not the scope of the program that is unique. Concerning training, Jack Stack notes that often when supervisors train employees they "fail to reach the highest level of intelligence of those people. We often fail to give them the best education; we shoot too low." He believes management should teach employees a basic understanding of the company, ranging from research and development to tax strategies.

SRC also uses other nontraditional training approaches. One such program is the use of "commodity" budgets. At SRC every supervisor is encouraged to take on additional responsibility in the form of these commodity budgets. In essence, each person is given responsibility to monitor and control a plant-wide commodity such as abrasives or chemicals. These overhead items become the exclusive domain of this person. If a person asks to monitor "chemical" overhead, he or she tracks all chemicals used in the plant, even including "white out" correction fluid.

This type of on-the-job training makes everyone a better manager because each has to learn to communicate and to seek cooperation from those not under their direct control. The thinking is, "I've got to persuade others to control this expense. If I cooperate with John, who is in control of abrasives, he will be more cooperative with me when I try to control my area (chemicals)."

As a result of this on-the-job training, personnel have to learn new areas, gain an organizational perspective, and develop a teamwork attitude. The direct benefit of this program is that everyone becomes better informed and is more likely to understand another point of view. Customer satisfaction is indirectly enhanced because employees understand how they affect the customer and how the customer affects them.

ROLE OF HIGH STANDARDS AND TESTING

Training and motivation are essential if front-line employees are to understand their role in developing customer satisfaction, but of equal importance is the need for tests and standards. American Express believes it owes much of its success in service to its emphasis on service testing and measurement. Statistics are tracked on over 100 service measures. In turn, these measures are tracked in every country in which American Express operates. Once the information is collected, monthly performance reports are issued to staff worldwide. These reports are then reviewed to determine ways to improve performance. American Express sets high standards. Any executive whose department performance is below 98% has to explain what went wrong and what he or she is doing to correct the problem.

Texas Instruments CRC experiences are typical of successful service operations. Like American Express, CRC finds it essential to set high standards for its service facility. Some of the standards include:

• 95% of callers get through on the first try
• Phones are answered on the first ring
• An average 4.5 minutes of talk time
• Queue time average is less than 30 seconds per caller

They also sample customer satisfaction and strive to accurately respond to inquiries within two hours.

CRC has been able to consistently meet most of these goals despite the fact that they deal with more than 300,000 products throughout 14 divisions. For example, 90% of the customers receive a satisfactory response within two hours: quite an achievement considering the magnitude of the job. The 800 number is available to the general public and generates about 1,000 calls a day.

The Pepsi-Cola General Bottlers of Springfield, Missouri, has the highest level of quality out of the hundreds of Pepsi bottlers in the United States. They are the only bottler to receive a 100% rating from Pepsi USA. This means that when samples of Pepsi were taken at the plant and local stores, there were no deviations from national standards. A key reason for this success is the insistence on and adherence to quality standards that are higher than national standards.

The Springfield Pepsi Bottlers' tests do not vary from national standards but the frequency of and dedication in performing them does. Inspections are almost continuous. Even if there are only five minutes remaining in the workday testing is still performed. One manager noted, "We want to instantly know if anything goes wrong." When asked why, another manager stated, "It's expensive but it could be even more expensive if a customer bought something defective!"

Many poor service companies lack a thorough inspection routine. The Pepsi-Cola General Bottlers know the importance of inspecting their product, showing the results, and following through on those results. In this manner it is possible to constantly remind the employees and management of the company's commitment to high standards in manufacturing and service.

Image is critical to the success of top level service providers. They maintain high customer satisfaction because they know the company's image and sales are built on strict adherence to quality measurements and standards. A fundamental principle of service is to assess what action is needed. Raymond J. Larkin, executive vice president of operations for American Express Travel Related Services (TRS) Company, has said, "The ultimate objective (of the quality process) is to make a science out of service and to make customer service requirements quantifiable" [1].

Chip Peterson, the director of marketing at Pepsi-Cola General Bottlers, said that everything about the product is watched constantly, and no compromises are made. He mentioned that they recently received a shipment of bottles that had tiny black specks embedded in the plastic. By the time this was noticed, 300 cases of perfect product had already been produced. Those 300 cases of soda were poured out because they did not meet the company's definition of qualitivity, and were potentially damaging to the Pepsi image. The marketing director went on to say, "When customers buy our product they know what it is, what it looks like, and even how it's packaged."

Pepsi's production manager also displays this perfectionist attitude. When an inspector from the Pepsi headquarters was taking samples he remarked, "Well, it's close enough." The production manager's immediate response was, "No! We want it exactly right, not on the low or high end!"

At Pepsi-Cola General Bottlers, high standards are not limited to production, because quality is also based in part on how the soft drink is displayed and rotated in the stores. The general sales manager emphasized, "Every account is served everyday. If there is a problem everyone will help. If needed, our CEO would run a route to make sure the product is delivered."

To help motivate personnel they use incentives (one which we will examine in greater detail later), and also keep records and note outstanding days. The sales manager tells all route personnel where they stand on a daily basis.

He makes a point of setting individual goals and compares present and past performance. He also makes a point of asking personnel what they want to accomplish next year and then identifies exactly what each employee will need to do to reach their individual goal. This process of goal setting provides a powerful incentive for front-line employees. Clearly showing these employees what is expected in the form of goals and standards is another common characteristic of exceptional service providers.

As might be expected, testing and standards also figure into Wal-Mart's formula for customer satisfaction. Usually, Wal-Mart checks its quality five or six times before a product is put on the sales floor. Three to five percent of the merchandise cases are checked at the factory to make sure they meet specifications. When a shipment is received at a Wal-Mart distribution center, five cases of each product are opened and checked. If there is a problem with quality consistency, the entire shipment is returned to the supplier.

Holiday Inn, Tandy, American Express, and Zales likewise enhance their customer satisfaction through adherence to strict standards. For instance, in 1986, 108 hotels were removed from the Holiday Inn System. The main reason revolved around failure to meet product standards. Zales, the retail jewelry organization, uses a Quality Control Department which inspects as many as 15,000 pieces of their merchandise, or 100% of all merchandise they receive through their Dallas Distribution Center.

Hallmark, the world's largest greeting card company, also uses extensive testing to ensure quality. Homer Evans, corporate vice president of the Cards Product Division notes, "Every design, every new idea must pass through a tough examination before approval." After cards are designed and the words chosen, Hallmark repeatedly checks to make sure that they meet specifications.

14,000 new card designs are produced each year and go through this testing procedure. Each card is processed through thirty testing stations before it is approved. At every station something new is added: a stock number, envelope size, type of fold, number of colors needed to reproduce the artwork, and so forth.

Testing and standards, as these organizations believe, are essential operational ingredients for effective delivery of services, but this alone is not enough to ensure consistent and responsive service. A true measure of an organization's willingness to invest in customer satisfaction comes from the top. Quality service is cultural. Any hope of ingraining this culture into the organization rests on the corporation's ability to raise quality assurance to equal or higher status with other operational, marketing, or financial concerns. We will briefly look at how two companies, Tandy and American Express, help create this cultural focus on quality assurance.

Tandy Corporation (the Radio Shack people), like the others, places a great value on testing and adherence to standards—and it has paid off for them. One interesting measure of their success is their dead-on-arrivals

(D.O.A.). These are items that are shipped and arrive at their destination not working properly. At one time Tandy's D.O.A.s, like the rest of the industry today, ran around ten percent. Thus for every 100 computers shipped, ten would not work. Now Tandy's percentage of D.O.A.s is around nine-tenths of one percent.

Like Hallmark and Pepsi-Cola General Bottlers, the reason for Tandy's success is emphasis on quality control standards and tests and a corporate focus on quality assurance. The National Quality Control (NQC) department is a corporate "watch dog" that tries to make sure all products sold in Tandy's stores meet their standards. Each factory has its own quality control department reporting directly to each plant General Manager. However, final testing is performed by the corporate NQC through visits to their own and vendors' plants. Pete Falcone, vice president of Quality Control, says that the purpose of the visits is to, "make sure plants do the things we want them to do because we (NQC) are their customers."

NQC has the authority to shut down their factories for both minor and major problems. To help NQC remain responsive, they operate an "Early Warning" system where they phone 50 of their stores each month looking for customer complaints.

Central to their efforts is the practice of implementing their standards and testing procedures. Pete Falcone related a story about Tandy using an outside vendor to supply them with a specific type of printer. In shipments of 50 printers usually more than twenty-five would fail incoming testing. Frustrated, NQC questioned another computer company using the same vendor and asked if they too were having trouble with the defective printers. The other company's representative looked surprised and said, "No! We don't test them. I guess if the customer has trouble we send someone out to fix them."

NQC inspects all merchandise they receive before it goes into one of the 7,000 Tandy stores. Nothing is shipped directly to the stores. All incoming shipments are held until the inspections are complete. They do a wide variety of tests, including vibration testing and environmental testing to shock the products to see if they can withstand extremes in temperatures.

Like Tandy, American Express' success with quality assurance is based on the important role it has within the corporate structure. American Express has a general manager in each country who is responsible for all business. Every discipline, including quality assurance, reports directly to the general manager. Thus, quality is of equal importance on the organizational chart as sales, marketing, and so forth. In fact, quality assurance at every level within the organization reports directly to the top executive of that unit.

Similar to Tandy's NQC, American Express' success at implementing these standards and measurements begins at the top. Quality service is a basic part of the structure of the organization. Everyone knows the interest corporate headquarters has in quality. To further clarify this position, on-site quality reviews are made by the vice president of Worldwide Quality Assurance for Travel Related Services (TRS). This vice president, along with other vice presidents of TRS, spends several weeks at a site looking at the whole or "holistic" aspects of quality assurance. This includes analyzing the marketplace, competition, operations, and systems. The vice presidents then make recommendations that will improve the overall service. The extensiveness of the review, according to the vice president of Worldwide Quality Assurance, is similar to a car manufacturer wanting to produce quality cars. To do that they might look at the entire process of acquiring materials, assembling cars, marketing them, selling them, servicing them, and so forth [2].

MANAGEMENT SUPPORT GROUPS

Developing standards and comprehensive, corporate-induced standards and testing produces better quality and, in turn, higher customer satisfaction. Likewise, management interaction with service front-line employees is central to customer satisfaction.

Texas Instruments CRC is different than most 800-number service centers which often only use one supervisor for every 100 telephone operators. At the CRC they have a supervisor for every 10 agents on the phone. However, it is not the numbers that are important, it's the relationship between management and employees that is important. Management at the center believes that supervisors should act as a support group for the people out front, so employees in turn can be a support group for their customers. The manager of the center, Georgia Kendrick, notes, "It's important that we try to keep their morale up." She went on to emphasize that service needs people-oriented supervisors. She said, "You have to respect and care for your fellow man and treat others the way you would like to be treated." The CRC believes all service needs "people persons" first before other factors are added.

This attitude of management acting as a support group is not exclusively limited to the CRC or to service. SRC makes a policy of treating their employees as equals. Mike Carrigan, vice president, said, "We set a corporate policy of open communication. We share everything." The result is knowledgeable and well-informed personnel who know management is behind them.

Management support is shown in many ways including, most importantly, a basic belief in the ability of their people. Sam Walton of Wal-Mart flatly states, "It's our people who make the difference and our attitude toward each other makes our people different."

Clearly, mutual respect for employees seems to be an integral part of good service. Raymond J. Larkin, executive vice president of Operations, Credit, and Quality Assurance for American Express TRS, has stated that there were three key reasons why American Express formalized and expanded its quality assurance efforts in the late 1970s. First, the company was expanding rapidly and felt it imperative to have a consistent quality process. Secondly, top management recognized that poor service and unhappy customers equalled lost revenue, and would negatively affect its growth and profitability. Finally, he stated they were convinced that "employees really wanted to do a first-rate job. If they were shown how to improve services, we knew they would be happier, prouder, more satisfied, and better workers" [3].

Of course, deeds are stronger than words, and these companies do back up their words with proof. As proof of managements support of their employees, Wal-Mart allows personnel a great deal of individual responsibility (73% of their merchandise is typically ordered by department heads rather than corporate purchasing). They have an extensive profit sharing and monthly recognition program. The reason, as one store manager observed, is, "Employee involvement is the key to the success or failure of any retail organization." It is management's responsibility to support their employees because if their employees are more interested in the company they are more likely to offer friendly service and find ways to increase productivity and profits.

Jack Stack, president of SRC, agrees about the importance of personnel. He has said, "We've got incredible people—every single one of them!" SRC knows customer satisfaction begins and ends with their personnel. Management here makes a point of getting to know their employees. They know all the employees on a first-name basis and know a lot about their personalities. They talk *to* them, not *at* them. There is an open door policy and employees are encouraged to ask questions. Upper management displays a sincere interest in the people and, most importantly, treats everyone as an equal. There are no titles here. Some companies see employees as a necessary evil. At SRC they believe in their people. Management believes employees are special, and in turn, employees return that trust and enthusiasm.

The Pepsi-Cola General Bottlers' Springfield, Missouri plant has an unusual way of showing management support. It might be called leading by example. Every key person within the organization started his/her career as a route salesperson, or came from the production line. Every manager drove trucks, loaded and unloaded supplies in stores, rotated stock, and directly dealt with customers. Domino's Pizza uses a similar approach with great success.

In the Domino's Pizza organization, management support occurs naturally because, "everyone starts at the bottom." They know their products and customers from the ground up. Employees know their bosses were promoted because they were the superstars. Here, if you want to be middle management you must start at the bottom. The consolation is that promotions come from this pool. As a result, many of their truck drivers have college degrees.

Management support is also seen in their attitude. As one manager mentioned, "Everyone works as a close-knit group to put us on top, no one pushes for sales and forgets products, profit, or control. Everyone knows you can only sell it once, so they had better do it right the first time." Other plusses to such a system are the fact that everyone keeps a consumer perspective, and the fact that it assures each manager has a clear understanding of the day-to-day business operation. Often, poor service providers are those whose management has little appreciation or understanding of what it takes to produce the services. Top service providers, on the other hand, have managers who know what their delivery system will and will not do.

SERVICE PEOPLE

Dedicated people with the right traits are crucial if a business hopes to obtain the quality service that in turn produces the customer satisfaction essential in a service society. The traits needed in personnel vary, depending on the business and the job. SRC prefers "competitive and hungry" people. Nordstrom, recognized by many as one of the best service retail stores, looks for "nice" people. Both of these companies are excellent organizations but with different needs. It seems clear that in addition to other traits, one common trait is extremely valuable to a service organization. When Texas Instruments CRC was asked what the foremost reason for their high customer satisfaction was, the response was "dedicated people." They emphasized that for service to be successful it takes someone who cares about someone else. CRC looks for people who really enjoy helping customers. They do not believe a "stop-watch" approach is in line with an emphasis on quality service.

The center prides itself on its dedicated people. CRC is able to get the dedicated people they have in part through an extensive and detailed interviewing process. Typically, they select one out of twenty interviewees to work at the facility. Jean Jones, department manager, noted that when employees are being interviewed they know they are playing with a pretty good team and that in order to play they have to be pretty good themselves. Thus they obtain dedicated people in part because they have high expectations. Management emphasizes that the job is not just answering calls, instead it includes projecting the right image to the customer.

The Texas Instruments operation obviously places a great deal of faith in, and credit for their success on, their people. They would get a lot of agreement from others who have been able to develop customer satisfaction.

While CRC is telling stories of how their people come to work despite personal problems, other service providers have just as much faith in their own people. American Express gives a variety of awards to front-line service providers who perform above the call of duty. They call them "Great Performer" awards.

Pepsi-Cola General Bottlers has just as much admiration for their employees. The director of marketing notes, "Our people have a lot of pride in what they do, they know what's in it for them." He went on to say that for many, their jobs were their whole lives. The production manager points out that his employees might go into a restaurant after work thirsty, but most would not buy a competitor's soft drink if the restaurant did not serve Pepsi. Other managers tell of how they receive letters from employees' wives saying, "We just wanted you to know that the kids and I really have a warm feeling for Pepsi." It sounds corny, but it is real.

All the other companies we have talked about in this chapter can relate similar incidents of employees being alert and preventing problems. Others tell stories of employees taking the extra step to ensure customer satisfaction. Still others tell of a crisis occurring and employees volunteering to come in and help without pay. Management did not have to ask, employees simply came in on their own. It is impossible to put a price tag on such loyalty and support.

KEY POINTS

The message is clear. If organizations want customer satisfaction they must be willing to invest in it. At the very least they must monitor customer preferences and desires to help ensure customer satisfaction. In many cases, just the effort of monitoring alone seems to improve customer satisfaction. There are always complaints, but if someone is listening it will improve customer trust and respect.

Training and motivation are essential for helping employees understand their role in developing customer satisfaction. An employee must have this background to prepare for the job. Only in this manner is there hope of long-term success.

An organization's commitment to setting high standards and implementing comprehensive testing is also critical to customer satisfaction. Customer satisfaction does not just occur. It takes close follow-up and a perfectionist's attitude. As the saying goes, "Good, better, best, never let it rest till your good is better and your better is best." All the companies discussed in this chapter have a strong desire to improve their services and products, but it is their effort at upholding standards that makes the difference.

A positive climate existing between employees and management is also essential. Employees are not a "necessary evil"; they are the solution to customer satisfaction. Service needs dedicated people. It is difficult, maybe even impossible, for employees to be unhappy on the job and still give the necessary effort to ensure customer loyalty. Management has to support its people so they in turn can support their customers.

Some key points to remember include:

- Make customer satisfaction a central focus at the corporate level
- Monitor customer needs, desires, and attitudes
- Involve upper management in monitoring and better understanding the customer
- Find and hire people who care about delivering quality service
- Focus efforts on training and motivation of front-line service providers and management so they know how, and why, to deliver services
- Expose personnel to a corporate-wide perspective
- Openly share information about the corporation and the need for service
- Show support for, and faith in, front-line service providers
- Provide testing and adhere to standards established
- Set high measurable standards on quality service (aim for perfection)
- Provide goal-setting and feedback on employee performance to standards

REFERENCES

1. Blickstein, Steve, "It's in the Cards," *The Quality Review*, Winter 1987, p. 8.
2. Rasmussen, MaryAnn E., "Ensuring Quality on a Worldwide Basis," *American Productivity Center Quality Forum*, July 14, 1987, p. 8.
3. Larkin, Raymond J., "The History of Quality at American Express," *American Productivity Center Quality Forum*, July 14, 1987, p. 2.

Chapter 3

Focus on the Customer

One of the first lessons to be learned from exceptional service providers is the need to focus on one's customers. Demographics change and so do customers' needs.

In 1980 the median age in the U.S. was 30. Demographers estimate that by the year 2000, as the baby boomers mature, the median will creep up to 40. Instead of the 18–34 year olds who were the standard household of the past and once (though no longer) the largest buying group, the new household consists now of people aged 35–50. By the year 2000 this age will nudge up to 40–55 year olds [1]. What will this mean for service businesses? Older people worry about health, physical fitness, and security more than younger ones. They have different interests, and they enjoy different sports.

Not only will we be older, we will be wealthier, and people will be more preoccupied with finances. Today, estimates show that the average total new worth of a household is a substantial $160,000 [1].

It is estimated that 60% of the households in the early 1960's were considered middle class. By 2000, the number will be reduced to about 35%. While the middle class declines, the upper and lower classes will increase, each accounting for about one third of the population at the beginning of the next century.

This three class society will demand diversity of services and products. Instead of all competing for a shrinking middle class, businesses will differentiate themselves and appeal to very specific market niches. Customized products and services will become ever more numerous. There will be more $100,000 cars as well as more $10,000 cars.

Ninety percent of women with children under age 6 will be employed [1]. Cooking, cleaning, and child care for dual-income families will more often be handled by a non-household member or a service business. People will continue to eat out. Kitchens will be meeting places and not just eating places. Frozen foods will be more popular.

28

Currently the average full-time job consumes 55 to 60 hours per week. Money-rich and time-poor people will want services we probably have not imagined. Primarily, these services will be designed to maximize the customer's discretionary time. We already have services to pick up our mail, deliver office supplies, run errands, and carry messages. It is possible to have someone actually come into your home and wait for repairmen, carpet layers, phone installers, and so forth. If you don't have time to wash your car, take it to inspection, or renew your license, you can readily hire someone else to take on these chores. Personal grocery shopping services and other pickup and return services will be increasingly more commonplace in the year 2000.

While all of this is happening, where is American business? Does it really know who it is serving? Will convenience continue to be a top priority of our customers? Do customers want services that give them more free time or do they want services that take up their free time? Will our customers desire means of enhancing themselves physically, psychologically, or, will a less self-centered philosophy develop? Do they want interactive entertainment or passive leisure activities?

Customers' needs are multi-dimensional and constantly changing. Demographics change and needs change. Businesses that are able to keep current and future consumer opportunities in focus are the ones who will experience long-term prosperity. These changes can present problems for organizations unprepared to deal with them, but they present real opportunities for those that recognize the changes. The best way business can protect its future is to focus on the customer and his/her needs. In the following discussion we will look at several organizations able to gain a real advantage over their competitors because they clearly kept their customers in mind when conducting business.

THE NUMBERS TELL THE STORY

Almost without exception, top service organizations have focused on customers. Typical of their attitude is Southland Corporation's distribution system. The proof of this is in the numbers that describe their business. Their distribution system has a 99.7% service rate. Thus, only three times out of a thousand are they out of stock. Typical of their success is the record for on-time deliveries of one of their Distribution Centers located in Fredricksburg, Virginia. That center has only missed a delivery four times in fourteen years of operation—each time because of snow. Perhaps this is one of the reasons sales to independent customers have been growing at about twenty percent per year. The distribution system is Southland's. Last year they shipped more than 1.5 billion dollars worth of merchandise.

The Southland Corporation of Dallas, Texas is the 12th largest U.S. retailer and the largest operator and franchiser of convenience stores. More than half of the U.S. population lives within two miles of a 7-Eleven store. There are obviously many reasons for their success but certainly one of those reasons is their distribution system.

Southland's distribution system consists of five distribution centers that supply 5,800 7-Eleven stores, as well as 3,300 non-Southland operations. Some of the operations they serve include national restaurant chains such as T.G.I. Friday, Show Biz Pizza, Chuck E. Cheese Pizza, Bennigan's, and Steak and Ale restaurants. They also supply more than 2,000 independent convenience stores. The distribution territory includes 41 states and the District of Columbia.

Southland's service rate and on-time delivery is impressive because it occurs despite several challenges that exist within their type of business. They offer their convenience stores a "broken case" distribution concept. This means that Southland distributes most of their products in less than case amounts. Thus a store can receive two bottles of ketchup instead of a whole case. A manufacturer may package items in cases of 48, but if the customer only needs two of the item each week, then that's all that should be delivered. Southland focuses on what customers want or need, not what the manufacturer wants to ship. The customer, not the manufacturer, dictates the amount.

While their competitors also individually "pick" items to be distributed, Southland does more of it. Of the 3,000 items in a typical convenience store, they pick and distribute about 2,400, or 80%. The nearest competitor individually picks about 400 to 500 items. The outcome of being able to deliver less than case quantities is that their convenience store owners have more shelf space for other items. Individually picking and distributing items has resulted in the typical convenience store being able to carry 500–900 more items than it previously could.

MARKET-DRIVEN ATTITUDE

One of the main reasons for Southland's success has been their philosophy toward customers. It might be defined as, "don't assume what the customer's needs are and what you should do to satisfy them; instead find out the true needs." Customers may want quality, price, accuracy, or some other aspect. Once the needs are clearly identified, then and only then, should you try to be the best you can at fulfilling those needs. It is a matter of customer fundamentals. The secret to Southland's business success begins and ends with their ability to focus on their customers. Dale H. Allardyce, Vice-President of Distribution notes, "Everybody is putting an emphasis on the home run—the spectacular play—and forgetting about getting on base. The latest technological gadget or that big contract will not help if you do not take care of the day-to-day business. If someone improperly packages material, or a driver gets into an argument with a customer, then you can forget it." This service provider has not forgotten his customers. Jere L. Lehr, Manager of Market Development and Planning Distribution Group, emphasized that they make sure to *keep in touch* with the customer. He said everyone from Account Management to Vice-Presidents spends a great deal of time in the field. The purpose is to try to find out what the customer needs. All their managers spend entire days working in their customers stores. On these visits they are looking at what created errors and asking what they can do to overcome those problems. This concept is similar to other service providers. Wal-Mart's upper management makes frequent visits to all their stores. Nordstrom, Domino's, and Pepsi-Cola General Bottlers of Springfield, among others, require all their management personnel to start at the bottom.

Several innovative companies even use their customer service centers to help them to stay in touch with their customers. Rather than have their centers simply be complaint handling centers, they use them to stay in touch with and improve relations with their customers. General Electric's main customer contact is their GE Answer Center. Many 800-number centers only answer calls during the normal work day. The GE center is open 24 hours a day, seven days a week, providing information about GE products and services. A third of their calls are prepurchase inquiries, a third involve product use and care after the purchase, and the last third involve service, including how to diagnose problems [2].

Polaroid's Consumer Resource Center (CRC) is an 800-number center used for consumer assistance. It handles 1,500 calls a day. Representatives have a lot of latitude to do whatever is necessary to make customers happy. Polaroid uses the center not only for customer service, but also as a marketing tool. They ask questions of all customers who own certain types of Polaroid products. The process provides feedback about the marketplace and particular issues of concern to the company. On the theory that a solved problem shows that the company stands behind its products, Polaroid also uses the center to cross-sell other products.

Both GE and Polaroid use the service centers to enhance the all-important image of the company. It helps them stay in touch with their customers' problems, needs, and desires. Surprisingly, it also has provided a means for increasing sales and improving marketing effectiveness.

The message is simple: stay in touch with customers. The Vice-President of Southlands Distribution recommends to be successful you must "try to keep a high level of exposure to your customers." According to Allardyce the key is to remember what need in the market you are trying to fill. He suggests that business ask itself why they are in business and focus on the answers. Identify the customers for whom you are trying to fill a need and, most importantly, how you can fulfill those needs better than anyone else in the marketplace. In short, by looking at your service in terms of price, quality, and responsiveness you can then determine what the customer wants. Having done this, then examine your available resources so you can best fulfill the need.

SERVICE ORIENTED

Southland Distribution and other service providers believe that their success has hinged on their ability to form a partnership between themselves and their customers. Allardyce said that Southland "could be a 'peddler' of groceries, or a partner in the customer's success."

They felt that to be more competitive it was necessary to provide merchandising assistance and service. They started with the assumption that they must provide competitive pricing and quality. Next they asked themselves what else they could provide that would give them an advantage over their competition. Such things as electronic order entry, high service rates, merchandising assistance, and other programs were designed to enhance their service image and customer loyalty.

It is clear that this organization has a consumers' perspective, perhaps because they are directly tied into the 7-Eleven stores. They know store managers are increasingly busy. Clerks must listen to gas pumps beep, see who is out there, keep the coffee hot, get someone a fresh sandwich, process a money order, check in a video rental, and even process a lottery ticket. These people are pressed for time and management knows it.

This company approached this problem by introducing one-stop delivery, in which they deliver all their products at once, rather than dealing with 15 to 20 separate vendors each week. The result was less distraction and less work for the clerk. Rather than stack all the supplies on a pallet that gets in the way of store customers, they use "roll in" carts that carry all the merchandise and can quickly be rolled out of the way until a clerk has time to deal with it. This objective is simple but effective, "make a customer's life more manageable, controllable, and profitable."

Neiman-Marcus is a national retail company with headquarters in Dallas. They also operate a mail order service that takes a consumer perspective. They use the center to enhance their image and also help make their customer's life more manageable. For example, whenever a customer receives a complex order such as custom engraving, they are asked to call the 800 number immediately if there are any problems. The telephone representatives also receive special product briefing about potential problems that might lead to unsatisfied customers. For instance, if an actual color of an item is different than what the catalog picture shows, representatives advise the customer when he/she is placing the order. Representatives also advise and help customers select clothes that coordinate, thus reducing returns [2]. Another way to increase the profits and loyalty of their customers is to *give them a piece of the action*. Southland did this through their policy on allowances and discounts. Frequently a manufacturer offers a distributor an allowance or discount on a product. Unlike some distributors, they pass a percent of the total purchase dollars back to their customer. For example, if a store buys $200,000 worth of product on which the manufacturer was offering a discount, the store could get back $2,000 to $2,500. In a 100-store chain that amounts to a $250,000 saving. This policy can be profitable to a small chain of independent stores. In the last seven years the distribution company has passed $63 million back to their customers in the form of allowances.

Seven years ago grocery stores had such systems available, but it was an innovation in the convenience store business. Southland also developed a system where a clerk could "read" bar codes from an order book. Once this was recorded, the data was hooked up to a telephone line with an 800 number that went into a computer receiver at a distribution center. Later Southland added bar coded shelf labels so products could be directly read off shelves. Again, this was common in grocery stores but not in convenience stores.

One final merchandising assistance technique also demonstrates their *customer-oriented focus*. Recently Southland introduced efficient shelf planning (ESP) for their customers. This is a computer program that evaluates a variety of products based on the sales volume, profit, and movement they generate. It then produces a "planogram" that shows where individual products should be located on shelves to maximize sales. The program also provides a graphic picture of how the items should be stacked, which can be redone to factor in new "hot" items, thereby improving the merchandising and reducing labor.

CONSUMER RESEARCH

Many of the innovative customer services that top service providers introduced were later adapted by competitors, but the innovators were able to gain an advantage because they were first in introducing a service. American Express, Federal Express, Holiday Inn, Domino's Pizza, and Southland Corporation are all innovators in their respective fields. They have all found success by focusing on developing new products and services, targeting new markets, and implementing new products to gain new customers.

American Express, like Southland Corporation, has a long line of service innovations that helped build their success. For instance they were the first to establish strategic partnership between U.S. and Japanese financial service providers. One of their more popular innovations involved developing a new type of credit card called Optima. *Fortune* magazine voted it one of the "outstanding products of the year" in 1987. The Optima card lets American Express card members extend payments on purchases at an interest "significantly" below that charged by most credit cards.

Other advances include the Purchase Protection Plan that insures most items bought on the American Express card against theft, fire, loss, or accidental damage. American Express also introduced an advanced computer system that improves the accuracy and speed of foreign exchange transactions.

Holiday Inn, Inc. is yet another service organization that has not only survived but become very profitable because of consistent service and innovative approach to service. They became successful through good business sense and, as with Southland Corporation and American Express, very intelligent use of consumer research. For example, in 1965, Holiday Inn was the first hotel to use computerized reservations. In 1977, they were the first hotel to guarantee all-night reservations. They were the first major hotel chain to offer a centralized payment plan for travel agent bookings. That same year they became the first chain to offer a room guarantee (i.e., your satisfaction is guaranteed or your money back). They were the first to introduce a frequent traveler program. Many of the industry standards such as free parking, free ice, color T.V., swimming pools, in-room movies, and children under twelve staying free were initiated by Holiday Inn.

Domino's Pizza is our last example of a service innovator that has had enormous success. Their reasons for phenomenal growth are discussed in some detail in a later chapter. Domino's success, like that of the other companies mentioned above, has been based in part on their ability to innovate. They were the first to apply a variable cutting machine (VCM), which is a blender-like machine used for cheese grinding, to the pizza business. They were first to use fiberglass trays for dough making. They simplified the dough handling and preservation process and were one of the first to use sturdy corrugated pizza boxes, portable car ovens, and the "ferris wheel" type of oven.

Southland Corporation's focus on research and development resulted in them being first to introduce a variety of products and services: video rentals, ATM, "Big Gulp," and so forth. More specifically, they were the first to design their distribution system for their customers. Research and development has helped Southland and other service providers to be at the forefront of customer service. The focus of their research, like that of other top service providers, is to identify customer needs. The Vice-President of Distribution at Southland Corporation remarked that they want to know what takes up their customers' time and what creates problems for customers. Once they know this then they ask what can be done to overcome those problems.

Since Southland, just like the others, kept in touch with their customers' needs, they knew what kind of services were needed. They knew many of their customers had a need to transmit information, especially to store headquarters. They knew their customers' headquarters needed statistics on daily sales, customer counts, per store averages, receipts, cash deposits, gas tank readings, and so on. Today, customers, as long as they have a receiving system and a personal computer, can use the order/entry system Southland provides to receive this information.

All of these organizations show a pattern of being innovative in their field. This constant exploration of ways to enhance their particular consumer relation is truly one of the keys to this and other quality service organizations' success. These organizations' ability to innovate in the area of consumer services has been their trademark. The success of their research is based on a thorough knowledge of their customers' needs.

Any good service provider continually experiments with expanding the boundaries of service to their customers.

Allan F. Jacobson, Chairman and CEO of 3M, succinctly stated the importance of innovation to customer satisfaction when he said, "There are only three issues critical to business success—innovation, productivity, and total quality." Why? "Because they're not programs imposed by management. They're demands straight from the customer." His company certainly knows the power of innovation. 3M generates more than 25% of its annual $8 billion in sales from products new to the market in the last five years [3].

APPROPRIATE TECHNOLOGY

The Vice-President of Distribution of Southland Corporation believes their most important resources are "customers and employees." They do not introduce technology just because it is available; only if there is a customer need which the technology satisfies. Vice-President Allardyce emphasizes that in addition to customer contact yes they also make a point of maintaining contact with support industries to see what is available. Specifically they are looking for ways to meet their customer's needs and make their corporation more productive and cost efficient.

Their ESP technology is an example of this type of research. Since it shows a store manager how to best place merchandise to maximize space, profit, and movement, it can be a real advantage to their customers, especially small-chain convenience stores that normally do not have data on market conditions. ESP eliminates the need to physically set up store shelves since the stock and display people can refer to the photograph. Because ESP accurately calculates dimensions, it lessens problems encountered in fitting items on shelves. Thus, ESP is not only a marketing tool for the corporation, but also benefits the store personnel because they can spend less time looking at records and trying to determine the best layouts for products.

The Southland distribution centers are experimenting with new technology, including flatbed scanners to improve quality control of entire orders by scanning unit-picked items on a random sampling of orders. Southland has computers in every one of their 45-foot tractor-trailer delivery trucks to monitor speeds, rpms, start/stop times, idle times, and warm up times. The system provides a performance evaluation of the equipment and driver, thereby reducing traffic cost.

Currently Southland is examining the possibility of satellite communication with delivery trucks to maintain constant communication and know where each truck is at all times. The reason for this is so they can call and give their customers a closer estimate of arrival time. An important point here is that the technology is not leading the service, it is the service that leads the application of the technology.

American Express is another organization that obviously does many things right. One of those things (like Southland Corporation) is make appropriate use of technology. American Express has enormous investment in technology. *Fortune* magazine [4] reported that American Express plans to spend $300 million on technology. It is an investment with a purpose.

They have an on-line computer management information system that shows each manager every error that surfaced in quality assurance sampling during the preceding 24 hours. American Express also introduced a communication system called 3-Sigma. It identifies the top one percent of the service performers and through scientific methods defines how they consistently meet quality standards [5].

American Express is also experimenting with expert systems that are being used to facilitate some repetitive and simple customer servicing decisions. Some of the expert systems have allowed them to achieve productivity increases on a ratio of 700 to 1 as well as improving the consistency of their decisions. They are using applications of Artificial Intelligence, one of which is called Authorizer's Assistant, a computer system that automates routine charge authorizations.

Other technological activities American Express is experimenting with include implementation of computer automation systems like those employed in microfilm record retrieval, consolidation of outgoing mail by zip code, and so forth. They use electronic imaging that helps improve processing, storing, and retrieval [6]. Even with all of this automation and application of high technology, they are able to maintain a service-oriented perspective. An American Express representative has been quoted as saying, "While we recognize the importance of technology, we always remember that computers don't deliver service, people do, one transaction at a time" [7]. Top service providers do not seek to automate, eliminate, and simplify, rather they seek to *improve service performance.* The focus is different and so are the results. Effective service providers let the service lead the technology, not vice versa.

KEY POINTS

The Vice-President of Distribution at Southland believes that the majority of the American population is disgusted and tired of the indifference and shoddy products they have to put up with as customers. Top service providers try to have their fingers on the customer's pulse.

The organizations noted in this chapter have been highly successful because they identified their customers' needs and tried to satisfy those needs. A long list of innovations and service-oriented behavior was created to satisfy the needs and wants of customers. It is a system that recognizes the necessity of forming a partnership between business and the consumer. They were able to form a closer partnership because they did not assume what their customers wanted. They ensured their success by making sure they stayed in touch with customers. The merchandising assistance, special allowances, electronic order entry, selling products in less than unit amounts, theft protection on credit cards, and guaranteed reservations all demonstrate awareness of customers' needs for improved services. Rather than buying technology for technology's sake, as many have, these companies made appropriate use of the technology because they keep in close contact with their customers. Focusing on the customer has improved profits and service of these organizations. Those service providers who want to be successful in the future should focus on their customers by doing the following:

- Don't assume customer needs, find out. (See service from the consumer's perspective)
- Stay in touch with your customers. (It will help you recognize your service opportunities and develop a closer partnership with your customers)
- Invest in customer research
- Use appropriate consumer technology. (Technology is only valuable if it addresses customers' needs)
- Communicate your (and your customers') desires to your personnel

REFERENCES

1. Sheth, Jagdish, "Search for Tomorrow," *Public Relations Journal*, December 1987, pp. 21–51.
2. "Increasing Customer Satisfaction: Through Effective Corporate Complaint Handling," U.S. Office of Consumer Affairs (Pueblo, Colorado: Consumer Information Center).

3. "Quality: The Competitive Advantage," (Paid Advertising Section), *Fortune*, September 28, 1987.

4. Uttal, Bro, "Corporations That Serve You Best," *Fortune*, December 7, 1987, pp. 98–116.

5. Blickstein, Steve, "It's in the Cards," *The Quality Review*, Winter, 1987, p. 8.

6. Spechler, Jay W. "Quality Tactics at American Express Southern Regional Operations Center," *American Productivity Center Quality Forum*, July 19, 1987, pp. 11–14.

7. "Streamlining Customer Service: American Express," in *Issues in White Collar Productivity*, Industrial Engineering and Management Press, Norcross, Georgia, 1984, pp. 61–63.

4

Dependability

The subtitle of this and the next chapter could be called "satisfaction guaranteed." This, among other attributes, is what these service providers have in common. Reliability or dependability from the customer's point of view must be more than talk. Some businesses talk about delivery "in about an hour," but if they really believe in it why do they not guarantee it? Guarantees that offer a 100% satisfaction guarantee of a business service or product are an extremely powerful way to enhance a business image as a dependable supplier. Offering such a guarantee entails responsibility. An organization must be operationally rock solid if it is going to be successful at offering these promises. The organizations in this chapter have that, and more. That is why they can successfully implement guaranteed satisfaction.

If one were looking for a business that represents the very definition of dependability, it would be extremely difficult to find a better example than L.L. Bean. When customers order from this outdoor specialty catalog company they receive exactly what they ordered 99.89% of the time. Some of the companies in their business have a one or two percent inaccuracy rate. L.L. Bean's dependability goes beyond merely accuracy. For one thing, they offer a 100% satisfaction guarantee, no questions asked.

The company also gets those 5.5 million orders out the door and headed towards their customers within four-and-one-half days. A 99.89% service level and rapid turnaround are no small accomplishments considering the volume and variety of the business they do. In 1987 L.L. Bean shipped approximately 10 million packages totaling $428 million in sales. In that same year they received 9 million orders and customer-service telephone calls as well as 5 million pieces of mail.

In ten years L.L. Bean's sales grew tenfold and the variety of items carried increased sixfold. During that time the number of employees only grew five-fold. L.L. Bean is an effective and efficient service provider and is considered the best in its field.

Here is a story of American success by insistence on quality service. Long before foreign competition, L.L. Bean had developed a formula that ensured customer loyalty and support. For instance, each year 3 to 3.5 million outdoor sportspeople make treks to the 50,000-square-foot store in Freeport, Maine. Many of Bean's customers send photographs of themselves wearing the products. Other customers call the telephone operators to ask for personal advice on matters such as what to name their hunting dog. One couple even got married in the store!

SATISFACTION GUARANTEED

Insistence on quality and the 100% satisfaction guarantee are as old as the company itself. If their founder, Leon Leonwood (L.L.) Bean, did not invent satisfaction guaranteed (Montgomery Ward did in 1872), he certainly is one of the people who perfected it. At the turn of the century, L.L. Bean had worked at various sales jobs in his twenties and thirties. He had always had a passion for hunting and fishing, and in 1907 was working in his brother's store but was more concerned with keeping his feet dry on hunting trips. At that time there were either leather boots or rubber boots. The rubber boots were dry, but cumbersome and difficult to wear.

L.L. Bean then hit on the idea of putting the leather uppers on everyday workmen's rubber boot bottoms, plus some other improvements. He tried them out and liked the results. He sold a few to his hunting friends and they encouraged him to sell them to the public. In 1912 at age 39 he got a mailing list, and made up brochures that in no uncertain terms stated, "We guarantee them to give perfect satisfaction in every way."

The test of that promise was soon to come. The rubber bottoms separated from the leather uppers in 90 of the first 100 pairs of shoes. Bean kept his word and refunded the customers' money. He then improved the design, borrowed some more money and mailed out more brochures [1]. L.L.'s initial approach of *personally testing* his products and keeping the customer satisfied at all costs started here and continued as his reputation and facilities grew.

In 1917, when he added knit stockings to his line of hunting boots, he only did so because he personally tested them and decided his customers would like them. This process of customer satisfaction was ingrained into the company by L.L. Stories are told of how he would react when he learned that one of his products failed. He would "charge around the factory" trying to find out what went wrong. He would then return the customer's money, write them a note, often enclose a gift, and sometimes even invite them to go fishing. When he died in 1967 at age 94, everyone knew that L.L. Bean thought of his customers as family.

L.L. Bean had an intuitive understanding of the value of reliability; thus the "unconditional guarantee." You could and still can today return any Bean product for any reason. Customers have returned products after they have worn them for a year. Stories are even told of customers returning products *years* after they were purchased. Some products were returned even though the company no longer made them. No matter—Bean's stands behind their products. They, like other top service providers, remain focused on their customers. They do anything to keep their customers coming back.

In 1951, to satisfy customers' needs, they started keeping the store open 24 hours a day, seven days a week. It has only closed twice; once for L.L.'s funeral, and earlier for President Kennedy's funeral. Keeping the store open every hour of every day of every year is only one of the ways they use to keep their customers satisfied.

They make a determined effort to appear as part of the family rather than just a business. Typical of this approach is the models they use in their catalogs. Unlike those perfect models that are typical of other catalogs, their models are their employees. It is an old-fashioned, even "down-home" approach. It is also one that endears them to their customers. Telephone operators for the company enhance this image by talking to the customers about pets, the weather, or anything else the customer wants to mention.

Their approach can best be summarized in L.L.'s own words, "Sell good merchandise at a reasonable profit, treat your customers like human beings, and they will always come back." For some, this style of dealing with customers may be a little too "down home," but for their outdoor-enthusiast customers it appears to be just right. It is not an approach that might appeal to all, but it is one that appeals to *their* customers.

Regardless of the style, one overriding theme is appreciated by all customers and that is the 100% unconditional guarantee. It is rock solid and so is L.L. Bean's reliability. However powerful this guarantee is, it must rest on a strong business foundation if it is to be successful. Most companies could not offer such a guarantee even if they wanted to. Companies often cannot offer such a guarantee because of inferior organization, products, or service. If a company is going to be able to successfully offer any guarantee, they must provide a reliable product and service and have a strong organization to back it up. A strong service organization rests on the application of some basic fundamentals.

PERSONAL KNOWLEDGE

One fundamental evident in strong service providers is their use of knowledgeable personnel. This theme runs throughout successful service organizations. L.L. Bean wrote, "The chief reason for the success of the business is the fact that I tried . . . practically every article I handle." He said if he thought a knife was good for cleaning trout it was because he had tried it out [1]. Personally testing products was and is an important part of the business.

In 1967, when Leon A. Gorman, L.L.'s grandson, took over the business after his grandfather died, he made some changes, but not about their emphasis on *personal testing* of their products. Gorman is given credit for revitalizing and updating the company's marketing and managerial style.

Like many entrepreneurs, L.L. Bean was not able to effectively delegate. In the 1950s and '60s the organization was drifting. It was still highly reliable, but it was not growing. Some products were out of date and advertising was repetitive. Gorman updated this process when he took over. He improved the pricing but still kept the 100%, unconditional, money-back guarantee. More attention was paid to media selection. They increased the advertising budget, but did not neglect the operational side of the business.

As noted, one operational fundamental that remained in focus was their insistence on managers having personal knowledge of their products. When Gorman took over the business, he was, unlike L.L., not much of a sportsperson. But he learned, and now is an active cross-country skier, fisherman, and duck hunter. The organization encourages all of its managers to become active in sports. Any manager can get an extra week of vacation to do product testing through personal use. On a more conventional level, L.L. Bean managers, like those at Tandy, regularly visit the vendors' facilities. They examine the quality, product development, and new technologies.

A competent core of managers and staff that have an in-depth understanding of their business products and services can overcome many business shortcomings. Unfortunately, this is sometimes a rare commodity in business but, as we will see, service and product-knowledgeable personnel are essential for dependable and responsive service.

Product-incompetent personnel are probably the single biggest reason why many organizations cannot provide good service. Product- and service-incompetent personnel are one of the key reasons why many companies are unable to implement a qualitivity strategy. For most customers it takes a great deal of thought to recall when they were last serviced by a clerk, reservationist, or salesperson whom they felt really knew the product or service they were selling. It has taken time and it requires continuing emphasis, but fortunately for L.L. Bean and other dependable service providers, *product-competent* personnel are a fact at these organizations.

PEOPLE, NOT TECHNOLOGY

Although it is doubtful, it might be possible for technology to be more important to a manufacturer's success than their people, but certainly this is not the case for services. If people cannot do it, machines surely cannot. Machines are the tools; it is the hand that holds the tool that is most important.

In the early days all of L.L. Bean's employees were friends and neighbors. Today the emphasis still remains on people, not machines. L.L. Bean's great efficiency has been brought about through their people. Technology may supplement their personnel effort, but only when it improves the service.

In the case of L.L. Bean and other corporations such as SRC, it is people that make a conventional warehouse and distribution very efficient. No amount of technology can overcome basic organizational and managerial weaknesses. Recent cases of technology-wise and people-ignorant automakers demonstrate this point. Not so surprisingly, great service providers do not always have state-of-the-art technology; rather, they have state-of-the-art social or people skills.

This *social technology* includes an emphasis on training. Walt Disney's emphasis on training is well known, but other service providers like L.L. Bean, Merck, Federal Express, and others focus on it as well. At L.L. Bean all employees, even if they are seasonal, receive up to one week of training. They review a film on the history of the corporation and receive instructions on how to do their job right. We will discuss this training in greater detail in a later chapter.

L.L. Bean also provides *employee feedback*. For instance, they make great use of bulletin boards that have letters of complaints and compliments from their customers posted on them. They use quality circles and the like to obtain employee suggestions and feedback.

Of course, there is more to using human resources than simply getting feedback; *personnel must care about the organization*. L.L. Bean, and most other strong service providers, develop that caring by caring about their personnel. They have a strong benefits package. Among other things, they offer a 33% discount on all employee purchases [2]. Employees receive Christmas bonuses that vary depending on the length of employment. Like Wal-Mart and others, their profit sharing program is for those who work 1,000 hours or more a year. It is significant since it can account for 10 to 20% of an employee's salary.

SMART USE OF TECHNOLOGY

People are most important to services, but that does not imply that it is wise to ignore technology. A company may not need to be on the cutting edge, but it should at least be relatively up-to-date.

As already noted in the previous chapter, exceptional service providers recognize the proper place for technology. They know it should be used to help make jobs easier, more productive, less redundant and repetitive. Computers at L.L. Bean, like so many other quality service businesses, have played an important role in improving efficiency. Thomas C. Day, Vice-President of Fulfillment Operations at L.L. Bean, was quoted in *The New*

York Times as saying, "My preference is to use the computer much more in work planning, control and direction of the manual effort and not to invest so much in machinery" [2].

Computers keep track of materials received from vendors. They print shipping labels and find the cheapest way to ship (Bean pays for shipping of its products, not the customer). Computers help select the best size and type of boxes, and calculate postage. Bean can ship 80,000 packages a day in part because computers tell those who fill orders the fastest route to follow when "picking" the merchandise.

Their Customer Service Department also uses computers to help them process 215,000 customer questions a year. They also continue to use computers to reduce the time needed to ship an order. Computer market research is used to help locate potential customers. The point is that they do use some technology—appropriate technology, and it is smart use, but not overuse.

Front-line service providers will always be more important than technology. Top service providers look at what their people do and then, and only then, examine how they can use technology to enhance that service. Some corporations look to eliminate people with technology, but successful service providers look to improve consistency, responsiveness, and dependability, through the technology. It is simply a matter of perspective. Some organizations see employees as the problem. Top service providers see employees as the *solution* to the problem. Quality service organizations know that people *are* the company, and they look at technology as a way to improve services and make service providers' jobs easier. Technology is a tool for people, not a tool to replace people.

OPERATIONAL MANAGEMENT

There is great variation in the amount of promotion or advertising that companies do, but one thing remains constant with exceptional service organizations and that is their emphasis on operational management. Byerly's (see Chapter 6), a very successful Minneapolis chain of eight grocery stores, spends almost nothing on advertising and uses the money saved to improve service. Instead of advertising, they employ a full-time home economist who answers questions and helps customers plan menus. Byerly's generally tries to emphasize quality service rather than cutthroat pricing.

On the other hand, because of the nature of their business, L.L. Bean must use advertising to find the customers. Once they identify their customers, they make sure that operational management keeps them. It means they give a lot of attention to filling customers' orders in an accurate and timely manner.

You already know of L.L. Bean's 99%-plus accuracy level. Southland Corporation and Federal Express also have impressive numbers. Their on-time delivery and "fill rate" are approximately 99%. As with Bean, this high percentage is due to effective operational management. At Southland, computers pick orders which are placed in tote boxes. Drivers then receive these orders in an organized and timely manner. Truck routes are designed by computer. Specific instructions are written so drivers are able to take the most effective route. Tote boxes are delivered with invoice slips and clerks simply check off items. Here, as with L.L. Bean, operational management is what produces the qualitivity improvements.

Certainly one of the things that has helped Wal-Mart become more profitable is their distribution system. Most retailers build their warehouses to serve their present stores. Walton built very large, highly automated and computerized warehouses, then built stores in close proximity to them. In most cases Wal-Mart stores are within a six-hour drive of their five warehouses. Normally they can deliver their goods from their warehouses to their stores within 30 to 48 hours. Computers and conveyor belts move the warehouse merchandise to trucks waiting at loading docks. Typically, 12 trucks must be loaded and leave within 5 minutes, so the next 12 trucks can be served. These warehouses load 55 to 65 trailers a day and handle 65,000 cartons per day. Their goal is to ship all incoming freight in two days or less, and most merchandise is shipped to their stores as soon as it comes into the warehouse. Some items, such as clothing and advertising, are unloaded directly on conveyors to be shipped out, thus saving double handling and lowering costs.

Good operations management also means that Wal-Mart pays a lot of attention to the quality of their products as well as their service. For instance, many quality service providers, such as Southland Distribution, Wal-Mart, and L.L. Bean, require checks and double checks of incoming supplies from vendors. They have an agreement that manufacturers pay for 100% inspection of goods if a problem is found with a shipment [3].

L.L. Bean, Solid State, SRC, American Express (see Chapter 8) and others know the value of *measurement* to improve services. They measure the results of performance, cost, and promotions. To provide such exceptional service also requires an excellent distribution system. Like Wal-Mart and Southland Corporation, L.L. Bean's distribution system is at the heart of their success. They ship tens of thousands of parcels out within a few days. They have 51,000 items in stock and orders are processed and shipped within four and one-half days.

CUSTOMER FEEDBACK

Dependability can only come when a business knows what and when to deliver services. L.L. Bean and others put great value in assessing their customers' needs (Chapter 7) and demographics. Market surveys are conducted to determine their customers' needs. This information is then used to identify a potential mailing list. They react to every customer request or complaint and even go so far as to post their comments on bulletin boards that are labeled "Messages From the Boss."

The same attention to *customer feedback* is true of Federal Express, American Express, and the other top service providers. Goals are set by the customer, then it is up to business to meet those goals. Top service providers first ask customers what their expectations are and then set standards and develop employee motivation, training, and incentives to ensure customer expectations and corporate standards are achieved. Everyone gives lip service to customer feedback, but only the top service providers actually do something about it.

KEY POINTS

Customers remember missed deliveries and other unreliable service, but sometimes it seems that management does not recognize the impact that such poor quality service has on their business. Highly dependable service providers like L.L. Bean know that their success from the beginning has hinged on quality. They have one of the best unconditional satisfaction guarantees available. Along with other top service providers, their emphasis on quality has made it possible to offer such a guarantee.

Dependable, high quality service is based on several foundations. Providers take the extra steps to satisfy customers, to make them feel a part of the family. Friendly service, however, does not ensure dependability or long-term customer loyalty. Unlike many product-incompetent personnel of poor service providers, personnel in high-service firms have personal knowledge of their products or services. They are their own customers.

Managers of highly reliable organizations have a strong sense of appreciation for people within their organization. The amount and sophistication of their technology varies from one high-service organization to another. At best, many use mid-range technology, some even use low technology. While the degree of technology may vary, one thing remains fairly constant; top service firms are highly people-oriented. Employees are brought into the service process, feedback is taken and given, and participation in the quality decisions is an ongoing process. In short, they take care of their people because it is their people that must take care of their customers.

When technology is used it is designed with people in mind. It is designed to take the drudgery, redundance, and repetition out of service. Technology used to enhance service should help make service jobs easier, more productive, and rewarding.

Quality service means delivering what marketing promises. Quality, measurements programs, distribution systems, and many of the operational issues we will discuss later are critical to quality service. The primary goal in developing dependable service is to stand behind what is promised and give satisfaction guarantees. To do this, it is wise to:

- Please the customer, regardless of his/her concerns
- Develop product-knowledgeable personnel and managers
- Provide employee training to do a quality job
- Give front-line service providers feedback on performance and reaction of customers to their service
- Have the customers set goals for the organization
- Design production technology to make it easier and more rewarding for front-line servers and operational personnel
- Develop operational systems to support the delivery of services and products (promise what you can deliver, and deliver what you promise)
- Most importantly, take care of your personnel.

REFERENCES

1. Gorman, Leon A., "L.L. Bean, Inc: Outdoor Specialty by Mail from Maine," *The Newcomen Society*, July, 1981, p. 11.
2. Prokesch, Steven E., "Bean Meshes Man, Machine," *The New York Times*, December 23, 1985, pp. D1–D3.
3. Skrzycki, Cindy, "The Rustic Pitch Pays Off in Catalog Sales for L.L. Bean," *U.S. News & World Report*, March 25, 1985, pp. 61–62.

5

Responsiveness

Few things are more irritating to customers than unresponsive service. For many customers, even if it is good service, it is no good when it is late. Few customers appreciate standing in line waiting to be served. Some service providers have recognized the value of responsiveness to their customers and have incorporated it into their customer service. Even fewer are so assured of their responsiveness that, like dependability, they offer "satisfaction guaranteed" if they fail to meet their customer's expectations.

The "one hour photo" stores' sincerity must be questioned if they do not "guarantee or your money back" when they exceed the one hour limit. Those that promise that you will be served "in about an hour" rarely offer guarantees. Talk is cheap. Truly responsive customer service must be measured in a service provider's willingness to stand behind their product or service. Satisfaction guarantees demand more from service providers, but they also prove a service provider's sincerity to back up the talk. It may require more of an organization, but the effort is well worth the cost. Responsive suppliers secure customer satisfaction and loyalty. The arrangement can be quite profitable for an organization.

Domino's Pizza is one company that does back up what they say. The corporate organization offers three dollars off any pizza if it takes more than 30 minutes from the time a customer places the order until it is delivered. Their satisfaction guarantee also applies to product quality. If for any reason a customer does not like the product, Domino's will replace it or refund the money. It is important to note that some franchise and local store operations go beyond corporate guarantees by offering the pizza free if it is delivered in more than 30 minutes. Their slogan is, "Fast, Friendly, and Free."

Domino's corporate success is due largely to their ability to be responsive. The corporation is the second largest pizza organization in the world, with approximately 4,500 stores. Pizza Hut has more stores, but Domino's sells more pizza. It is quite an accomplishment for an organization that started in 1961, but as late as 1970 had severe indebtedness of about $1.5 million owed to some 1,500 creditors—and only 42 stores.

Many stories have been written about their plight, but basically it resulted from a mistake in changing the franchising and managerial policies that had led to their early success. We will review this point in a moment. These organizational problems were corrected, and by 1977 Domino's had resolved most debt problems and had 159 stores in 18 states with sales of $30.7 million. In 1982 the number of stores had jumped to 831, and by 1985 it stood at 2,000 stores with $310 million in sales. In 1987 Domino's had more than 4,500 stores and was growing rapidly. This is truly a remarkable accomplishment for an organization "that only sells pizza and coke;" no salads, no liquor, nothing but pizza and coke. Furthermore, there are no sit-down restaurants in the Domino chain of stores. They offer walk-in and delivery service, and about 95% of their business is delivery.

Their formula for success is a lesson well worth learning. It is one that rests largely with their ability to be responsive and to understand their customers. If we define service in part as guaranteed speed, then it is hard to find a better example of an organization that responds to customer needs and offers a satisfaction guarantee if they fail to meet that standard. Of course, responsiveness is of little value if the service is not reliable. As one franchiser noted, "We got to where we are because we were quick and reliable. Service is our ace in the hole." Their corporate service rate for delivering their product to customers within 30 minutes, year round, is approximately 92%. Marty Prather is one franchise owner who meets this service standard and has delivery times that average about 21.5 minutes. The national average is 23.3 minutes.

KNOW YOUR BUSINESS

Marty Prather, who has been a past "national manager of the year" for Domino's, mentioned that there are four things that you have to do for Domino's from day one. He said, "You're never going to make it if you cannot: (1) answer the phone, (2) make a pizza, (3) cook a pizza, and (4) drive/deliver a pizza." At first it sounds simplistic, but it is not. One of the foundations of this as well as other service organizations' success is their ability to quickly respond and their emphasis on managers totally understanding their business. Their managers are "working managers" who must know or do each of those four tasks. Those four jobs are critical.

One of Domino's (and other responsive service providers such as Federal Express) great strengths has been the fact that their managers and franchise owners truly understand their business. The vast majority of Domino's managers and franchise operators started out either as a driver or working in the store. Until 1969, Monaghan, the organization's founder, awarded franchising rights only to employees who had worked their way up through the system from driver to trainee to manager and so forth.

Many of the problems with debts incurred in 1970 and 1971 can be attributed to changing the franchising policy and opening ownership up to managers of other more established restaurant chains. Personnel started entering the organization who did not understand the customer nor the "responsive" fast food business. When they began bringing in professional managers with little grass-roots appreciation of the business, its customers, or its capabilities, the problems were amplified.

As noted in the previous chapter, time and time again successful service businesses are grounded in solid fundamentals. It seems that those who succeed and remain responsive as well as dependable have their fingers on the customer's pulse, know what their customers want, and know how to get it out of their business. To get this effort out of the business, managers must understand the operational aspects of the business. Those that are only grounded in financial or marketing aspects cannot understand what can and cannot be done. Almost without exception, the best service providers depend on fundamentally sound operational managers. They understand the substance of the business. All too often, college graduates assume they will start in a mid-level position where strategic, rather than operational, decisions are made. In reality, the better their understanding of the operational area the better they are able to formulate strategies and provide services.

Federal Express, as well as Nordstrom, Pepsi Cola General Bottlers, and Domino's, among others, develop this operational perspective within their managers by promoting from within. For example, at Federal Express 70% of the positions are filled internally and several of their vice presidents began at the bottom. Most of Domino's upper managers began their careers at the bottom, developing a first-hand knowledge of customer relations and business operations. Generally, today you cannot buy a Domino's franchise. Normally one must first become a store manager before becoming an owner. Of course this grass-roots management style is not necessary to develop the operational perspective, but it is necessary to set up some means of exposing personnel to the real challenges of day-to-day operational problems. In this case, promoting from within has helped their managers keep a "front line" perspective. They also use a variety of ways to keep in contact with their customers.

DEVELOPING A CUSTOMER'S PERSPECTIVE

Like Domino's, Federal Express, which began operation in 1973, is a modern-day success story that was built on responsive and dependable service. This "absolutely, positively overnight" express mail business has made many lists of best-managed businesses. Today they employ 63,000 people, and handled over 226 million packages and documents in 1988. Their service level is impressive. In 1987, 98.8% of the time their flights arrived within 15 minutes of scheduled times. Like other dependable and responsive suppliers (L.L. Bean and Domino's Pizza), they offer a "satisfaction guaranteed" for delivery of their services.

One of Federal Express' reasons for success, like others we have discussed, is their ability to get close to and focus on their customer. Their couriers are encouraged to get to know their customers. Stories are told and awards are given to employees who take the extra step to serve the customer.

One story demonstrates this emphasis on focusing on the customer quite well. It seems that a courier's van broke down while delivering packages. The courier, with the customer in mind, was able to get a buddy to help him push his van so he could deliver the packages to the customer. What makes the story unusual is that Federal Express employees are not supposed to push vans. However, the employee had assessed the situation, and asked the question, "What's it going to cost the customer?" He made the decision, and later got an award. By recognizing and encouraging such entrepreneurial spirit, Federal Express is further encouraging individuals to demonstrate initiative, responsive service, and a clear focus on the customer.

Focusing on the customer is as fundamental as you can get. Domino's Marty Prather recommends that managers keep in close contact with their operations by using some of their off-time to just sit in their store lobby and look at the facility from the customer's perspective. Managers may discover housekeeping problems or problems with their employees' appearance that could affect the image customers have about the establishment. To enhance their perspective, some managers go over to a friend's house and place orders. As this demonstrates, if a manager wants a true perspective of how assistants handle their tasks he or she does not sit and watch them because everyone will usually do a good job. Instead act as the customer, and judge performance based on customer perspective.

Domino's, like most responsive suppliers, does not simply rely on these informal means, although they are obviously important. One of their formal programs used to obtain a customer perspective is their Mystery Customer Program.

As the name implies mystery customers are just that. Store managers do not even know who they are. They order a product once a month and the corporation pays for the order. Two customers per store are supported by the corporation. In addition, many of the more successful franchises use an additional three or four customers per store. Since the average pizza costs about $7.00, that is a sizeable investment in customer feedback. Nationally that would be:

4,500 stores × 2 customers = 9,000 × $7.00 = $63,000 per month

Again, some owners, like the A&M franchise in Missouri, also include their own mystery customers in addition to those covered by corporate headquarters. This is done strictly to obtain more accurate feedback.

In return for delivery of a free product, mystery customers are asked to fill out a twenty item questionnaire that assesses the quality of the service and product. Questions relate to how customers were dealt with on the phone, i.e., were they put on hold; whether personnel were courteous and well informed; and if the product was delivered on time. There are also questions about the driver's appearance, attitude, and about product quality, i.e., temperature, toppings, flavor, price.

The focus remains on the customer's perception. If a product is late, as it is one or two percent of the time, the customer receives a three dollar discount, if not a free pizza, an apology card the next day and one dollar off their next purchase. Store managers also must make a customer callback. They want to make sure the driver was friendly and did not get mad because he or she had to give away a free pizza. In short, if something goes wrong Domino's wants to make sure it gets corrected and their customers remain pleased with their service.

Computer technology is also used to improve customer perceptions of personnel. It is not technology for technology's sake; rather, as in other cases we have looked at, it is appropriate use of technology to enhance the human performance.

Federal Express is one of the service providers that makes an enormous investment in technology designed to improve service. For example, they employ a "SuperTracker" that enables them to improve responsiveness. They recognized that as more and more customers became accustomed to overnight delivery, a way was needed to improve services. Their SuperTracker program helps customers have immediate knowledge of the fate of their package. Through the use of bar codes and computer technology Federal Express is able to tell their customers, within hours, where their package is anywhere within the delivery system. The company uses this technology and others, like their automatic call routing system, to quadruple their delivery (more than a million packages a day) while improving their service levels.

Domino's makes similar use of appropriate technology. For instance, every day Domino's receives a printout that shows when pizzas were ordered, what time they left the stores and when they arrived at the customer's location. Since the managers have worked in various positions within the store they know from personal experience what the system is or is not capable of doing. If products are leaving every ten minutes and they are being delivered late, they know it is a delivery problem. If they are leaving every 25 minutes, then they know it is an operational problem (scheduling, staffing, etc.).

Holiday Inn in 1965 made this same appropriate use of technology when they developed the first computerized reservation system, Holidex. Its purpose was to reduce customer check-in time. It also allowed customers an opportunity to make lodging arrangements more efficiently and quickly. It can handle 66 messages per second for fast, reliable reservations. American Airlines' Sabre reservation system, an industry innovation, also is appropriate because it makes customer interaction easier and faster.

STANDARDS AND IMPLEMENTATION

For managers to know their business and develop a customer's perspective certainly is important, but if a business is to remain responsive, there must be *standards of performance* and some way to implement those standards. Service standards are of little value unless they are supported by an infrastructure that focuses personnel, publicizes those standards, then stands behind them and rewards those who implement them.

Management has to make a commitment to their employees as well as their customers. Unless they are willing to stand behind the words little can be achieved. Guarantees to customers need to be made. Standards need to be publicized. Performance standards need to be posted for all to see if they are to be effective. For example, Domino's posts their service figures on the number of late deliveries where all can see them. A late delivery is one that was delivered beyond the thirty-minute deadline. Other key indicators, such as labor percentage each store ran, what kind of food sales ran, and whether those figures are up or down over the previous period are also posted. In a later chapter we will look at how American Express, a top service provider, uses standards to enhance their service.

Domino's, like Federal Express and others, also *monitor* their standards closely to make sure they are achieving their objectives. For instance, in order to help monitor their 30 minute guarantee, Domino's provides each driver with a digital watch which is synchronized with the store's computer time. The purpose is to enhance their responsiveness and image. A driver greets customers at the delivery point and tells them the time on his/her watch, which matches that at the store. The time it should have taken is also posted on the pizza box. Theoretically all three times, the delivery person's watch, store watch, and time on the box should be the same. When drivers return to the store they "call out" the time of the delivery so *immediate feedback* of the system's performance is available to the manager. Based on this information changes can be made in various operational aspects.

This company also provides *awards* and *rewards* whenever their standards are exceeded. This might include giving an award for the fastest delivery time. For instance, since they want their drivers to hustle, some stores give them "hustle bucks" that can be redeemed for money. Hustle bucks are intermittent rewards that managers give, at their own discretion, to those who look like they are hustling. This might include those who jog in and out of the store and so forth.

Federal Express also uses performance standards to help improve responsiveness and quality of service, but they had to be careful in using them. Unless a business is very careful they may encourage the wrong things. Sending "mixed signals" is worse than not sending them at all.

At Federal Express they do monitor phone calls as many other service centers do, but performance rating is only part of the evaluation. They discovered that it was better to "take care of the customer" than to set a standard of 30 seconds on the phone. Mixed signals hurt service. If the standards are set up based strictly on speed and a "quality interface" is expected, then the company is sending mixed signals. One manager at Federal Express noted that when they told employees to take care of customers and reduced the emphasis on purely statistical performance measures, performance actually improved.

Standards should be challenged, and most effective managers will ask themselves, "How can we do better, where can we be better?" This takes more than simply keeping track of average performance. Speed can only come when personnel understand their customers, know what their system is capable of doing, and then find ways of getting more out of it. Of course, standards and awards help but without *systematic incentives* (see Chapter 10) very little long-term improvement can be expected.

Training, along with incentives, is important if service is to be responsive. One manager at Federal Express said, "If you take care of the people, you get service." This process begins with training. For instance, at Federal Express customer service agents go through an extensive five-week training period. It is designed to improve service so agents can answer any question a customer has. It includes classroom work, on-the-job training, and interactive television where agents first must provide the right answers before going to the next step. Some of the skills emphasized, beyond technical matters (rating packages, etc.) include how to problem solve and how to empathize, not sympathize, with customers. In reference to the latter, they want agents who understand the customer's point of view, but not to the point that they get so involved that they cannot solve problems.

Trainees and store managers at Domino's constantly receive training on various aspects of their business. This often includes training at the store and at the "pizza college." Store training includes such areas as how to drive, answer phones, how to make dough, etc.

Domino's also has a pizza college where it is possible to pick up a bachelor's degree, master's degree, and even a Ph.D. in pizza management. Courses include personal goal setting, personal money management, time management, and how to dress for success. Other courses cover stress management, evaluating trainees, and exposure to the corporate philosophies and values. Of course, Domino's also focuses on customer relations and how to effectively manage the "team members."

SPECIALIZATION AND SIMPLICITY

Responsiveness, like so many other positive service attributes, rests on the foundations of good business principles. However, that alone is not enough to ensure responsiveness. One characteristic that seems especially relevant to an organization's ability to be responsive is the need to remain fairly *simple and specialized*. The simpler the organizational design, product, and service, the easier it is to be responsive. It is still not an easy task, but at least the organization is designed correctly.

For instance, Federal Express has only five levels of management from top management to lower level operational personnel. This is a remarkably "flat" organization considering its sheer size. Domino's is the essence of simplicity and specialization. As noted earlier, they sell only pizza and coke. There is no sit-down service, only pick up and delivery, and 95% of that business is delivery. While some fast food restaurants have diversified their menu, Domino's has not. As one franchise owner noted, "If we ever do start delivering chicken, it will be a completely separate organization." While this remains to be seen, it is clear that they are adamant about the need for simplicity in order to be both responsive and successful. They learned this lesson the hard way.

When Thomas Monaghan started the Domino's organization in the early sixties he focused on making pizza, rapid delivery, and simple services. He originally had a partner in those early ventures whose operational philosophy differed from his own. The partner implemented soda fountains, french fryers, steam tables, and grills. In other words, he wanted to set up a traditional sit-down restaurant. The approach was not distinctive or unique and it certainly did not help promote the initial successful strategy of "fast, free, and friendly" service. Monaghan wanted a simplified menu, but his partner wanted regular restaurant menu items.

For three or four years the business suffered from this split personality. Finally, when Monaghan did split with his partner their organization had serious debt problems that almost destroyed it. It was only in 1965 when he removed the sit-down tables, reduced the menu and returned to operational simplicity that Domino's profits also returned.

Monaghan set up a *centralized facility* to prepare the pizza ingredients. He thereby simplified the production process since employees at the store only had responsibility for assembling and cooking the products. He introduced the fiberglass tray for dough making to the pizza business, and pioneered sturdy corrugated pizza boxes and portable car ovens.

With this focus on simplified products and services, he was able to develop a strategic niche by offering fast, free service with a minimum of overhead. There are no waiters, except for drivers, and no sit-down service. They only need a 1,000-square-foot building rather than the traditional 2,500 to 3,000-square-foot building. There is no need to worry about atmosphere. The focus is on efficiency. This distinct and simplified strategy is what makes Domino's fast and effective.

Today their stores remain fixed on that strategy of making pizza quickly and getting it to the customer fast. There is very little to divert the manager's attention, unlike the traditional restaurant manager. For example, there is very little concern for location, usually a critical factor for most services. Today even their main successful competitors, like Pizza Hut, have found it necessary to open up separate units that only deliver. Now when a customer orders from Pizza Hut, the food comes from a different location than the one where customers dine when they go out to eat. Needless to say, these "delivery only" Pizza Huts normally do not match the "red roof" image most customers associate with Pizza Hut.

Using a simplified structure, like Federal Express and Domino's, is at the heart of many responsive service providers. Mini Maid Services, the highly successful Marietta, Georgia based maid service, also depends on simplification for their success. Leone Askerly, owner of the company, when asked the secret of her success responded, "We do one thing, one way, for one price" [1]. She went on to say, "We arrive with a smile, we have knowledge, we deliver what was asked, and we call back new clients the next day to see what could be done better."

Despite a *simplified structure* and focus, there are still ample opportunities to get distracted. Marty Prather at Domino's noted that even when a small change was implemented in their system some problems developed. Recently they introduced a centralized phone center rather than a phone at each store. It soon became the "phone center against the stores and vice versa." Whenever wrong addresses were typed each would blame the other. Problems were solved when store managers were brought to the phone center and operators brought to the stores so each could see how the other operates. Both developed a better understanding of each other's perspective and problems.

The problem was two distinct types of operation. One type involved sitting down and taking orders, the other revolved around making pizza and sending it out. Neither group knew the other's problems and headaches. The phone center people did not see the store computer printing out order after order. Store managers did not realize the problems and hassles the phone personnel were going through with wrong numbers, not knowing where the customer was, and the customer telling them the wrong address (sometimes on purpose). Obviously if a company that is built for speed and simplicity can develop the problem of losing focus, then almost any organization runs such a risk. It takes a great deal of cooperation, communication, and commitment to ensure that the focus remains on responsiveness.

KEY POINTS

Responsive service organizations, like dependable ones, have certain key characteristics. Customers who receive unresponsive and undependable service often complain because what they thought they would get and what they got were different. Responsive organizations, such as Domino's, L.L. Bean, and Federal Express, among others, let their customers know what they will get and then back up their words with a satisfaction guarantee. They promise to be responsive or your money back!

It is a promise they keep about 99% of the time. It is a promise that is possible because they have certain abilities that most companies do not have. It is possible because they have applied some basic fundamentals necessary for running an effective organization. It is also possible because they are clearly focused on providing responsive service.

These organizations do not lose sight of the fact that they are guaranteeing speed and, as such, have developed a simplified and specialized system to deliver it. While these service providers' success rests on a foundation of good management, their efforts must be focused on the unique aspect of their service that differentiates them from other services. In this case it has been speed that was guaranteed, but other service qualities like accuracy, personal attention, or comfort could also be emphasized.

As these organizations have demonstrated, in order to be responsive or deliver quality service, it is necessary to totally understand what the business is and is not capable of doing; then do it. Management and front line personnel have to understand both the capabilities of their system and what customers expect from it. While marketing and financial knowledge is of obvious help, it is operational knowledge that delivers the services and spreads the word of mouth about a business' dependability and responsiveness. It was the beacon that kept Monaghan of Domino's afloat in troubled times, and it is the single most important characteristic of effective service providers.

In addition to understanding the ins and outs of a business is the need to know one's customers. Customer feedback through direct or indirect means is critical, even though it may be painful. Complaint forms and the process of complaining should be easy. Unlike most companies where the customer has to be aggressive, service management should be the aggressor. They should aggressively seek, even solicit, customer input, suggestions, and complaints. If customers demand to "see the manager," management obviously has not done its job. Management should insist on "seeing the customer"— Mister Average as well as Mister Grumpy.

As noted in the previous chapter, making appropriate use, not overuse, of the technology is important. It is wise to neither become enamoured of nor resistant to technology. Federal Express' SuperTracker, Domino's synchronized watches and American Airline's Sabre reservations are all technology tools designed to improve services and responsiveness. These are all good uses of technology because they are designed to improve the service (in this case, responsiveness) rather than simply to replace people. Generally speaking, if you want to improve services, technology should be used to enhance personnel's performance, not eliminate people.

Finally, responsive management includes developing and implementing clear standards. This includes several elements that we will discuss in later chapters, including focusing management's and employees' attention on standards, rewarding adherence to standards, systematic use of incentives, and employee training to ensure that plans are converted into action.

In summary, some essential elements needed to provide responsive service are the need to first make a stand, pledge satisfaction guaranteed, and then back it up in the following ways:

- Build a grass-roots understanding of how the business is run and what its capabilities are in all personnel who must provide responsive service
- Get to know and understand the customers and what responsive service means to them
- Develop an entrepreneurial spirit among personnel rather than focus on policies (see Chapter 11 for more information)
- Use technology that enhances performance
- Set performance standards and implement them (Chapter 8)
- Provide feedback on performance
- Provide proper training to ensure that personnel can be responsive (Chapter 9)
- Make use of systematic incentives (Chapter 10)

- Develop a simple system that specializes in providing responsive service (the more items on the menu, the larger the variety of customers served, the slower the service).

REFERENCE

1. Russell, George, "Where the Customer is Still King," *Time*, February 2, 1987, p. 57.

6

Uniqueness

It would be fantastic if service organizations were able to be totally dependable, responsive, accurate, and able to consistently offer 100% total quality service. Even if it were possible, it would not be feasible. Even if feasible, it would not be smart. Some services are high cost, low return. For example, for two-income families, weekday deliveries of services are useless, and generally very expensive for a business. Useless or unwanted services are worse than no service at all because they divert resources away from other areas—areas that the customer would appreciate.

Variety, or lack of it, is a fundamental difference between services and manufacturing. Manufacturers can make a variety of products, but service organizations have a great deal of difficulty providing more than one type or level of service. As Domino's clearly demonstrates, their success, like many other service providers, depends in part on their ability to clearly focus on one direction and one type of service. Southland Corporation's Distribution System, L.L. Bean, and Byerly's, who we will look at in a moment, were successful partly because they were able to focus on one segment and then serve those customers exceedingly well.

In Southland Corporation's Distribution System case, the customers were the convenience stores they served (as opposed to the supermarkets that most distribution systems served). L.L. Bean's customers are the outdoor enthusiasts. Domino's near-tragedy clearly shows what can happen when a business develops a "split personality" and tries to serve two divergent groups. Federal Express went through similar problems with their ZAP Mail. As we will see, successful services develop a unique service concept that gives them a competitive advantage over the competition.

WHAT DO CUSTOMERS WANT?

It is up to management to identify customers and then assess what it is that those targeted customers want. Unfortunately, more often than not, what customers want and what management thinks they want varies greatly. For instance, many managers wrongly assume what customers want is cutthroat pricing when often what they want is an "enjoyable experience." Not surprisingly, many top service providers have been successful because they made their particular service activity unique and not simply the normal drudgery that most services seem to be.

Applying a unique perspective to their service is exactly what Byerly's has done. The result, like the results of Southland Corporation Distribution and L.L. Bean, has proven very profitable.

As already noted, Byerly's is a Minneapolis-based chain of grocery stores. In February 1987, they were featured in *Time* magazine as an example of a highly successful service provider [1]. Their approach to the supermarket business is truly unique. Unlike most supermarkets, they rarely advertise and instead, "spend the advertising money on service."

The difference does not stop here. Instead of the "smelly" grocery stores, with the cold and unappealing appearance that most are familiar with, Byerly's has chandeliers and carpeting throughout. There are no distasteful smells here. They use colorful wallpaper and have wide aisles. In fact, the stores look more like upscale department stores than grocery stores.

They do not offer trading stamps or discount pricing. What they do is place special emphasis on *customer service and helpfulness*. For instance, they employ a full-time home economist to help customers plan a variety of home and food-related activities. They color code their shelves so customers can find items that are appropriate for their unique diets. Yellow tags denote those food items appropriate for fat-modified diets, green tags are for gluten-restricted diets, pink is for diabetic or calorie-controlled diets and blue for sodium-restricted diets. They provide over 1,400 recipes "perfected in their kitchen" and have a wide variety of grocery items ranging from eggs to exotic and gourmet foods.

What they offer the shopper is a unique shopping experience. Some refer to it as "upscale," others call it a "dash of snob appeal." Whatever the interpretation, it has been very successful. To help ensure this unique appeal, each store is even managed semi-independently so store managers can gear their grocery items to the neighborhood where they are located.

The ability to develop this special image and appeal is due to focus. Everything is aimed at developing the right approach. Byerly's has the wide aisles, soft lighting, carpeted floors, and other upscale interior touches because these fit the approach. Even their grocery bags have a designer flair.

No brown bags here! Their stylish bags are blue and gray and embellished with Byerly's signature.

Like so many other top service providers, Byerly's approached their business from an entirely different viewpoint, unlike that of many service firms. Don Byerly, president of the organization, said, "The whole idea is to make grocery shopping fun, interesting, and less of a chore" [2]. A story in the *Wall Street Journal* noted that the atmosphere is so serene that some customers find themselves prolonging their visits. One customer noted, "I made my wife quit shopping with me because we spent so much time in the store that we were wasting all Saturday morning" [2].

CONVENTIONALITY

So what is wrong with being conventional? Why make yourself special? Conventional is another way of saying average, and average is a dangerous place for a business to be. If the majority of potential customers see a business as only average, and if they cannot see any important differences between one business and another, then that cannot be good news. Where is the customer identification? With little identification or loyalty there is no compelling reason for customers to return. Why should a customer pick one place over another if there is nothing unique?

For long-term success a business must differentiate itself from others. To ensure customer loyalty, as Byerly's and other top service providers have done, it is necessary to be able to offer the customer something special. Every one of the top service providers has something unique to offer their customers. It may be guaranteed responsiveness as with Domino's and Federal Express, or dependability as with L.L. Bean, or even consistency, as with McDonald's. Others may focus on convenience, spontaneity, attentiveness, or any of a wide variety of service attributes. Regardless of the service message, each should emphasize a firm's distinctive attributes.

To be unconventional or distinctive in the customer's eyes, it takes a different approach. Uniqueness and bureaucracy are on the opposite ends of the spectrum. Bureaucratic organizations rationalize and regulate. They develop policies, procedures, and rules, and try to eliminate all forms of frontline judgment, creativity, and initiative. Unique organizations recognize responsibility for customer service must not be limited to the customer service department (often where many incompetent employees within some organizations are placed).

Unfortunately, the approach many services are taking is the same one manufacturing took at the turn of the century. Taylorism, job specialization, and excessive division of labor are fading from manufacturing, but remain entrenched in the service sector. Highly-specialized white collar and service employees working at increasingly more specialized tasks is a fact in many service organizations.

Unfortunately, many service firms also fail to differentiate themselves from others in their field. Such non-service attitudes are seen in those organizations that over-serve a broad market, thereby operating with higher costs than necessary. This provides potential competitors with an opportunity to serve only certain market segments and operate at lower costs. This is what Michael Porter, a Harvard professor and renowned writer on the subject of strategic management, calls a *cost focus* strategy [3].

A similar unproductive approach is when an organization underserves a certain market segment either because they aim at too broad a market or because they are large and some segments do not match their economies of scale, so those segments are passed over. When this occurs, it provides an opportunity for a smaller competitor to fill a market niche by providing this market segment with excellent service. Porter calls this a *differentiation focus*. L.L. Bean, Federal Express, and Byerly's are good examples of this approach.

Domino's Pizza and SRC appear to have combined both of these strategies, which is truly unusual. Domino's cost focus is illustrated by their limited menu and spartan facilities. SRC's high ratio of direct to indirect labor, and high productivity likewise demonstrate their cost focus.

The differentiation of each firm can also be easily seen. Domino's was the first to exploit the delivery segment of the pizza market, and is still the only one to guarantee a speedy delivery. SRC's reputation for high quality and warranties that meet or exceed new-product warranties clearly differentiates them from others in their field.

The following figure illustrates the dangers of *not* developing a unique service philosophy.

The dish-shaped curve in Figure 6-1 demonstrates that some firms are low-cost leaders serving a broad market segment. As such, they serve a large market share and their low cost and high volume give a high return on investment (ROI). Wal-Mart is an example of such a firm.

Others use either a cost focus or a differentiation strategy that serves a relatively small market segment (small market share). By serving this segment extremely well they can command a higher price and thereby achieve a high ROI. In short, they are small and mighty.

On the other hand, many firms are "stuck in the middle" with only modest market share and below industry average ROI. This is because they try to serve the large segment of the market, which is already better served by the cost leaders, while trying to compete for some of the specialty markets which are well-served by the focusers. As such, these firms in the middle blur their image and compete poorly in all markets.

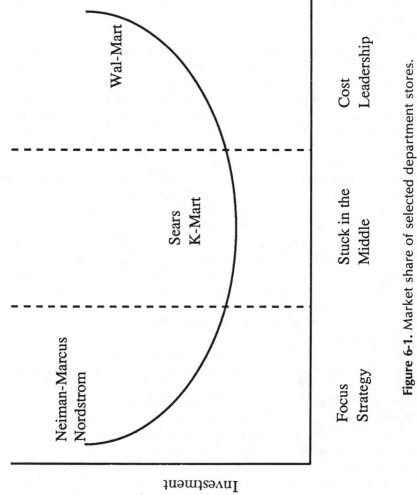

Figure 6-1. Market share of selected department stores.

Firms in the middle may have gotten there by once being successful as cost leaders, or they may have been focusers who got greedy and decided to go for other markets. However, being a market share leader does not guarantee ROI or operational success. Anything can happen to change a market and make it unprofitable or cause it to fade from popularity. This is why it is extremely important to stay close to the customer (Chapter 3) and remain very sensitive to environmental changes.

We will look at how to change some of these non-service philosophies to service philosophies in the remaining chapters. For now, though, we can begin to examine some basic ground rules for developing a *service perspective*: one that helps an organization differentiate itself from its competitors.

ASSESSING DISTINCTIVENESS

In developing a distinctive or unique approach, several things must occur. First, there is a need to *assess* where a business stands in relation to its competition. This is such an important issue that it is dealt with in a separate chapter. For now we can note some essential ingredients. It is important to find out what potential customers consider important. Then and only then is it possible to find out how a business meets or does not meet their expectations.

A business must assess demographic factors of potential customers, including age, education, income, family size, and so forth. More important are the "psychographic factors" of customers. This refers to the way potential customers think and how they act based on what they think. As we noted earlier, it is necessary and wise to get close to the customers and focus on them continually. Managers should see their business, as the Domino's manager does, from their customer's point of view. Assessing customers' preferences and attributes is a common characteristic of top service providers.

The needs of every group of customers vary, but most customers have at least one thing in common. *Perceived risk* (economic, medical, legal, and social), or rather lack of it, is the basis for many of the successful service providers. Research has shown that customers associate risk more highly with the purchase of services rather than goods [4]. The satisfaction guarantees offered by Domino's, Federal Express, L.L. Bean, and Wal-Mart help reduce such perceived risk. Customers often think they have less information about services so the satisfaction guarantee becomes even more important.

Of course, satisfaction guarantees are not the only way to reduce perceived risk. Customers often feel that they never know what to expect. Most would probably agree with the Holiday Inn slogan that states, "The best surprise is no surprise at all." Although certainly not perfect, consistent service is what McDonald's, L.L. Bean, Southland's Distribution System, and

Domino's have in common. These organizations understand that customers often feel that they have less knowledge about services than they do about products, so anything that improves consistency improves quality.

Beyond perceived risk, services must answer two basic questions. First, what do customers really consider important? Second, how does a business stack up against the competition? The answer to the first question comes from customers' attitudes and preferences. As already mentioned, those that focus on customers are able to understand and anticipate what their customers want. The answer to this, as will be seen in the next chapter, comes through a variety of means. Usually, the more numerous the assessment tools, the better.

The second question that must be answered is how does an organization stack up against its competition. This answer comes from within rather than from outside. Management must address two basic operational issues. They must determine any unique *capabilities* that differentiate them from their competition. Secondly, if there are unique capabilities, management must determine if they are being communicated throughout the organization and within the marketplace. The bottom line is that management of service organizations must develop a distinctive approach to their business, then, through effective management, make sure personnel and customers understand those differences.

DEFINING UNIQUENESS

Implementing an effective service strategy consists of such things as assessment, developing standards, training for personnel, using incentives, and so forth. However, before one can implement a strategy one must develop a unique service strategy. There are really only four distinct ways a business can make itself unique. According to Laurence Ackerman, a principal of Identica, Inc. in New York City [5], they are:

1. Proprietary means
2. Innovations
3. Developing new features on existing services
4. Reinforcement of time-tested, well-ensconced products

Proprietary, or at least close to proprietary, programs are one way an organization can be distinctive. This approach is perhaps the easiest one to understand. Whenever a business has exclusive ownership of a product or service, then it is easier to be distinctive. Such "proprietary information" is often protected by copyright or patent. Sometimes a service organization is able to develop a procedure or device so unique that it is patentable.

Expert systems and high technology allow companies to develop their own unique services. As already mentioned, American Express, along with many lab and medical organizations, is experimenting with such expert systems as Artificial Intelligence (A.I.) programs. These A.I. programs help credit authorizers decide whether to approve cardholders' purchases. They hope to use these A.I. systems to improve human judgment.

Such A.I. and expert systems allow machines to assume greater decision-making capabilities over simplified and routine services. Such appropriate use of technology should add greater variety in other tasks because it eliminates some of the repetitive nature of services, thereby enhancing the quality of work and, in turn, the quality of service.

A second way of making oneself unique is through an organization's ability to *innovate*. As previously mentioned, top service providers like Southland Corporation's Distribution System, American Express, Domino's, Holiday Inn, and American Airlines have been extremely successful through a wide variety of innovations. Innovations like American Airlines' Sabre Program and Southland Corporation's unique distribution system, as well as Domino's simplified production process, have helped them each to become industry leaders.

Usually such innovations are based on a thorough understanding of customers' needs and assessing the organization's ability to help satisfy those needs. Such truly new services take considerable thought and preparation. If an appropriate amount of preparation does not occur, one runs the risk of introducing programs no one wants or ones that are not cost-justified.

The third way of making an organization unique is by *adding new features to existing services*. Domino's "30 minutes or free" delivery approach is one such example. Satisfaction guarantees are another. Basically an organization, though still offering the same service as other organizations, finds a new wrinkle in how it is offered. For instance, a few years ago Holiday Inn introduced their "forget something" program. If travelers forgot to pack some of their personal toiletries, the hotel would provide complimentary items like toothpaste, shaving cream, shampoo, etc. Another strategy used was their "guest of the day" program where one guest was selected for special treatment including upgraded accommodations, fruit baskets, complimentary drinks, etc. Other special programs included those aimed at people registering alone; they were invited to join the manager on duty for breakfast or dinner.

Continually reinforcing time-tested services and products is the last way to make an organization unique. AT&T's Reach Out and Touch Someone campaign, and the promotional money used to insure that the public continues to use the service, is an example of this approach. Needless to say, Domino's, American Airlines, and others make ample use of this technique; however, like others they do not limit themselves to only one technique. As many techniques as possible should be explored.

All four of these techniques require Research and Development (R&D), developing a consumer perspective and knowledge of the business' true capabilities—not what they wish their capabilities were. Many would like to offer a satisfaction guarantee, but many organizations simply do not have the ability, personnel, capacity, or operational skills to be able to do it. Service organizations from churches to railroads can advertise all they want, but unless they understand our changing world and its needs, there is little chance for improvement. Reinforcement does not mean stagnation; even the most time-tested service must change with the times.

MAKING YOUR BUSINESS UNIQUE

All of these approaches should be considered when developing a service strategy. If an organization already has unique capabilities, they should be exploited and communicated within and outside the organization. However, after assessing internal strengths, it will often be necessary to develop human and other capabilities. Chapters 8 through 12 describe various ways of improving capabilities to ensure quality service, but each organization must decide what particular strategy should be used.

The service strategy may involve some of those already discussed or it may center around such strategies as attentiveness, accuracy, problem solving, and so forth. Depending on the approach, one may need to improve screening and selection of personnel, provide better scheduling of people or other resources or even better monitoring of services. As we will see, in most cases services depend on people and, as such, often better service means treating organizational members better, with increased respect, authority, responsibility, and autonomy.

KEY POINTS

The remaining parts of this book deal with implementing quality service, but those techniques will not be effective if an organization does not first sit down and determine exactly where they are going. Management must first decide what they want to be to the customer and what customers' needs they hope to satisfy before they implement any technique. Once these strategic decisions are made, then management can identify, apply, and evaluate techniques for achieving quality service.

Rarely, if ever, do service organizations do all things well, so they must choose carefully what service they can offer. Successful service organizations have identified those elements that they believe important (dependability, responsiveness, etc.). They have concentrated their efforts and made investments in those areas.

Once their service target is identified, they make a point of *effectively delivering results* that were promised at a 99%-plus satisfaction level. They make sure that standards are set, people are trained, efforts are encouraged, and organizational systems are in place to promote their service. The main points when developing a distinctive service strategy are to:

• Focus efforts in one direction and on one approach.
• Determine what customers really want (helpfulness, fun, etc.).
• Reduce your customers' perceived risk through satisfaction guarantees or consistency.
• Assess where the business stands in relation to its competition.
• Develop unique capabilities through proprietary, innovative, or other means.
• Communicate uniqueness to employees.
• Communicate uniqueness to customers.
• Improve capabilities (human and otherwise) if uniqueness does not exist.
• Decentralize management to meet unique needs and preferences of customers in varying geographical, cultural, and social areas.
• Encourage individual front-line initiative, judgment, and creativity.

REFERENCES

1. Russell, George, "Where the Customer is Still King," *Time*, Feb. 2, 1987, pp. 56–57.
2. Ingrassia, Lawrence, "A Bag From Byerly's is the Stylish Place to Stow the Garbage," *Wall Street Journal*, June 4, 1980, p. 1.
3. Porter, Michael E., *Competitive Strategy: Techniques in Analyzing Industries and Competitors*, The Free Press, New York, 1980.
4. Guseman, Dennis D., "Risk Perception and Risk Reduction in Consumer Services," in *Marketing of Services*, James H. Donnelly and William R. George, (eds.) (Chicago: American Marketing Association), 1981, pp. 200–204.
5. Ackerman, Laurence D., "What Makes Successful Service Companies Distinctive," *IABC Communication World*, Volume 3, October 1986, pp. 16–18.

7

Assessing Service

Before a business can begin to focus on its customers it must first understand who its customers are and what services are needed. Effective service providers know expensive service activities are of no value if they do not satisfy the customers' needs.

What organizations need to emphasize are those services that endear them to the customer and build patronage. Consumer loyalty is increased when customers expect and receive certain rewards. Rewards the customer seeks may be speed of transaction, attentiveness, dependability, consistency, or even excitement. It seems pointless to offer services unless there is a clear understanding of the customers' needs. Some organizations "think" they understand their customers, others think their customers needs do not change, and some just hope potential customers need their services. All of these attitudes are extremely dangerous.

Every firm needs to assess service provided to customers. Of fundamental importance is the need to assess the state of service and what improvements are needed. If there is no way to assess the service then there is no way it can be improved.

Assessing services has generally lagged behind assessment in the goods-producing area in part because it is fairly easy to measure the qualitivity of manufacturing tangible products, but not so for services. We obviously know when we are producing good or defective products but it is not that easy when discussing service.

Exactly what is quality service? It seems to vary depending on who you ask and from what perspective you are looking. For instance, what does quality health care mean to you? It depends on whether you are talking to physicians, patients, hospitals, health care administrators, or even family members of patients. Furthermore, services consist of many more intangibles than manufacturing. Mental activity is a part of many services but impossible to measure. How do you measure cooperation? You do not measure intangibles but, as you will see, you can at least measure the outcomes of service work.

Unfortunately, because managers are often unfamiliar with assessment of services, it may not be done. Likewise, because services have not been measured in many areas, mistakes sometimes occur. One mistake made by service occupations and organizations attempting to measure their work is that often managers in these areas rely too much on subjectivity or general impressions.

When managers assume that good service is a reality in their organizations, they run a real risk of making critical mistakes. Frequently many service occupations and managers become caught up in the day-to-day running of an organization and lose touch with their customers. In such cases what they assume their customers' needs to be may vary greatly from the actual needs.

Despite problems of assessing services, more and more assessment is occurring. There is really no choice. An organization must find ways of assessing their services because their competition surely will. We can now examine several ways service providers are assessing their quality of work.

CUSTOMER SURVEYS

American Express and other top-level service providers use customer surveys to help them assess performance. At American Express each month a summary of these findings is presented to the CEO. He, along with other personnel, then analyzes it to see where improvement in service can be made.

Customer surveys can be vital even for small organizations. Smith-Glynn Callaway Clinic in Springfield, Missouri reported that their surveys, along with strong financial and strategic planning, were the keys to their success. The clinic has a 42% overhead which compares with a 50–52% overhead for similar clinics. This lower overhead is significant since each percentage point translates into about one million dollars.

Effective financial planning does not make them unusual. It is their *sensitivity* to their patients and their attitude that separates them from most clinics. The doctors recognize that a great deal of their business comes through referrals and "word-of-mouth" so they try to manage their patient-customers in a professional manner.

Most clinics have risk management programs to make sure employees, patients, and legal aspects are reviewed, but it is highly unusual to see a physican's clinic worrying about customer satisfaction. The manager of the clinic believes patient satisfaction is one of the keys to their long-term success. This consumer attitude of the clinic is best summarized by its CEO who stated, "No phone rings three times here." They want their patients to remember the clinic's pleasant and professional atmosphere. To help determine how well they are accomplishing this objective, they have a nurse or other employee *randomly interview* patients and record their answers.

One area where the CEO feels fortunate is the physicians' attitude at the clinic. He noted the clinic physicians' positive attitude about change, stating that they "are receptive to change" even though they may not fully appreciate the business aspects of medical practice. Obtaining the cooperation and participation of physicians is a necessary part of an administrator's job. He noted that he has known many capable administrators who were not running profitable clinics, in part because of the physicians' attitudes toward their own productivity and business matters.

He noted that in many cases physicians' productivity is the "weakest link" in effective management. He mentioned that changing the work patterns of doctors is a difficult task. To help meet this challenge, as well as help encourage quality service by physicians, he relies on physicians' "peer pressure." Professionals should, and usually do, have some type of *self-policing* program to regulate physicians who deliver poor service. To encourage this self-policing, an income-incentive formula is used. After all of the bills are paid, approximately 80% of the distributable income is set aside based on the physician's productivity, 4% is based on seniority, and the remaining 16% is divided equally among stockholding physicians.

To further encourage self-policing, the CEO feels it is important to have doctors who appreciate the business aspects of clinics. To accomplish this he makes a point of "identifying problems, then documenting and sharing this information with the Executive Board." The purpose is to get their attention so they can begin to appreciate how their own quality care and productivity affect the success of the clinic.

In addition to providing comparative information, such as the number of new patients seen by each doctor, the CEO suggests that service providers, in this case physicians, develop a greater awareness of business matters. Therefore this organization has a policy of providing "free" trips to conventions for its physicians. The clinic pays for their doctors to attend meetings, such as those held by the AMA having seminars on business matters or changes that are occurring. Exposure to these meetings helps the doctors develop an appreciation of business, quality, and service aspects of medical practice. Once doctors appreciate these factors, the credibility of managers is enhanced and their job of keeping the clinic profitable and providing quality service is easier.

This clinic's approach to service is both innovative and heartening, but probably few companies put as much thought into customer surveys as American Express. Personnel at corporate headquarters track their system-wide performance at delivering services through their service tracking report (STR). The STR consists of statistics that track more than *100 service measures* relating to customer satisfaction. For example, they track to see if their centers are meeting their promise to replace lost or stolen cards within 24 hours. To ensure accurate information they track every card replaced.

STR results also are used to identify and assess service problems. If performance is not up to standards, quality assurance managers look for possible explanations. Once those are identified, local management must develop step-by-step action plans to correct service deficiencies. Progress on implementing these plans must be reported monthly. As part of the STR tracking and assessment process, effective solutions are shared by the quality assurance staff with managers in different locations who have common service problems.

Informally, American Express also assesses customer performance by *simply listening*. When corporate officials perform on-site business reviews of their various operating centers, a lot of time is spent listening to customer calls and reading customer letters. They also devote considerable time to listening to employees [1].

American Express' newest assessment tool measures customer satisfaction one transaction at a time. Their transaction-based surveys focus on how customers feel about *every single contact* [1]. They try to find out the customer's opinion of their product (card), as well as the customer's overall opinion of the company. Other information collected includes the customer's intent to renew membership, future usage, and word-of-mouth recommendations. American Express believes these transaction-based customer satisfaction surveys bring them closer to customers.

SELF-ASSESSMENT SURVEYS

There are many ways of assessing customers' needs, one of which is the customer survey. Many industries also make use of professional market research surveys. The objective is to try to analyze current service so it is possible to target ways of enhancing it. To be truly successful at this process it is important to *clearly define customer expectations*. The more clearly defined these expectations are, the greater the likelihood an organization will be able to identify a way of satisfying those needs. The organization will want to use as many methods as feasible to try and specifically identify their customers' needs.

Embassy Suite Hotels, a subsidiary of Holiday Corporation, helps motivate performance through self-assessment. In the employees' lounge managers post a daily report on the hotel occupancy rate, average room rate, and estimated profits, along with comments from at least five customers interviewed at random the day before [2].

Market research is good and so is asking customers to voluntarily fill out "comment cards" and other customer questionnaires. However, valuable as these methods are, they may not completely define the quality of service offered by an organization. Self-assessment surveys provide another means of determining if acceptable service is being provided. To make the most effective use of the survey it is necessary to make sure each question corresponds to some aspect of service that is important to an organization. If these areas produce low scores then you can identify measures to correct each weakness.

Each self-assessment survey can be aimed at a specific area within the organization. Individual departments can use it to assess service that relates to their area. Such a process can help analysis of and decisions in individual areas so improvements can occur. The most difficult issue to resolve, as with many assessments, is how to insure objectivity. Self-analysis, if it is to be effective, needs to be as objective as possible. Analyze service as it exists, not as it is supposed to be. For this to occur there must be trust and respect between management and the front-line service providers. It is a team effort and no punishment should occur because of a self-assessment.

ESTABLISHING PERFORMANCE CRITERIA

Another method of assessing customer service is by establishing some internal criteria affecting service (based on what the customer thinks is important) and then measure an individual, department, or organization's performance against that criteria. Thus accounting, computing, sales, and other services could be judged based on their contribution to the quality service of an organization.

One of the more interesting cases where this is occurring involves the measuring of white collar and service personnel at Solid State Circuits. This printed board manufacturer evaluates a wide range of measures. They assess everything from the typical production concerns to the more unusual concerns involving paperwork errors. Regarding these more atypical concerns, Tom Kowalski, the president of the company, said, "We started looking at how many errors we had in paperwork that feeds the production system. When we began monitoring paperwork mistakes the error rate declined remarkably. People know we were measuring the accuracy of our input because the results were posted for everyone to see."

At the heart of all of their systems is a concern for *nonconforming costs*. The price of nonconformance is what it costs to do things wrong, resulting in losses of money, time, or opportunity. Nonconformance costs include scrap costs, cost of working overtime due to producing defective products, expediting, bad debts, rework, or any other items associated with not conforming to requirements. When they totaled up these costs, Solid State Circuits found that thirty percent of their sales dollars related to these nonconforming costs. Thus if they had $16 million in business, thirty percent, or $4.5 million in cost was because they did not conform to requirements (i.e., scrap, rework, overtime, etc.).

There are also "costs to conform" to requirements as well as "costs of nonconformance" but the emphasis is on reducing the latter. Cost to conform includes such things as keeping the process running, calibration, audits, and use of quality assurance techniques such as statistical quality control. One manager mentioned that a small cost to conform expense can often offset a much larger cost of nonconformance. He said it was analogous to a taxi driver going to the wrong side of town (nonconforming cost). If he had bought a city map for $1.50 (conforming cost) it would have saved him a much greater nonconforming cost (i.e., gas, lost time, lost fare, etc.). The sum of nonconformance and conformance costs equals cost of quality.

Before Solid State Circuits began their quality improvement and assessment process, which also includes an extensive employee education program and revamping their corrective action procedure, 37% of their revenue was tied up in these costs. In less than a year this percentage had been reduced to around 17%. Therefore, for every $1 million worth of product they have a cost of quality of $170,000 rather than the $370,000 they had before this process started. A graph showing their improvement over the last year (1987) is seen in Figure 7-1. They have also reduced overtime by fifty percent. The focus here will be on how Solid State Circuits successfully installed various "white collar" or service measurement systems as part of their overall Quality Improvement Process.

Improving Sales Productivity

To enhance their productivity and quality Solid State decided it was necessary to measure service and white collar production as well as the more traditional blue collar production. They felt that to be successful, everyone, regardless of occupation, must get involved in the corporate goal. The sales department got involved by identifying and charting a variety of measures that relate to the effort to control nonconforming costs.

Dennis Stead, Vice President of Marketing, mentioned that one area they watch closely is *on-time delivery*. Each day the Marketing Department receives reports about completed jobs that were shipped to customers. They check to see whether the order was early or late (nonconforming) and record it on a chart. For instance, if an order was three days late it would be charted as a minus three. At the end of each day they determine how many

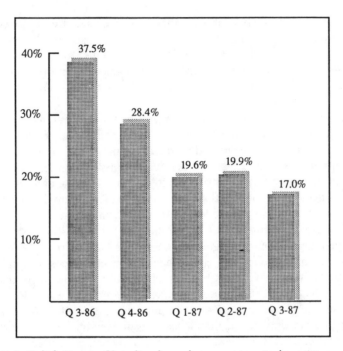

Figure 7-1. Solid States Circuits, Inc.; improvements in cost over previous year.

jobs out of each area were late or early and then record that number. At the end of each month, the monthly average for each area is recorded on their bulletin board. Their service goal has been to reduce these late shipments to zero. Within one year they have reduced late shipments from 12.5 to slightly over three days late.

Another customer service measure used by the sales department is *turnaround time on quotes*. All requests for price quotes from customers come to the sales department. They have a goal of four days from the time they receive a "request to quote" until it is typed and returned to the customer. Since the introduction of the charts they have consistently stayed below their goal.

Turnaround on change orders refers to when customers call in to reschedule their orders. When Solid State started charting and posting this turnaround time they established a goal of one-half day or less for rescheduling an order. Within seven months they met their goal and today the time has been reduced to two-tenths of a day.

Although Solid State Circuits uses other customer service measures, one of the more interesting is *nonconforming calls*. If a customer calls in and asks why an order is late, it is recorded as a nonconforming call. In other words the company did not conform to their customer's requirements or standards. Likewise when a customer calls up sales and says, "We are having problems with some product that you sent us," that is recorded as a nonconforming call. The sales department total goal is not to have more than five nonconforming calls a day. Since they began charting these calls they have begun dropping below the five-a-day goal.

They have been able to improve their quality service and reduce the number of nonconforming calls through several means. They reduce them by calling the customer whenever they know there is a potential problem rather than waiting for the customer to call them (nonconforming call). This procedure gives customers a better opportunity to plan so they do not have to simply react to an emergency. Customers may not like hearing that an order is going to be late but it is better than being surprised.

As one salesperson noted, "Before, if a customer called and said an order was late, that was the first we knew about it. Now it's better. Even if we don't catch all problems, we can at least be better prepared." As already noted they have reduced the average number of days late per month from over twelve to less than four days per month. The main reason: "We're doing it right the first time, closing orders short whenever possible. By being informed, watching the customers orders, and charting the changes, we keep the customer better informed."

Process Control

Process control monitors the flow of customer orders. They produce a report that identifies all jobs within the plant and at what stage they are in the production cycle. If there are errors on this report such as an incorrect job number, customer number, quantity, part number and so forth, then the sales and production managers do not know the true status of work.

The errors on this report relate directly to the quality of service because production and sales must use it to relay information to the customer. If information on the report is incorrect then it could result in late jobs and customers calling and asking, "Where is my order!" (nonconforming call). Since these errors affect overall quality they are being charted.

Accounting

Among other assessment measures, the accounting department measures and plots their *accounts receivable*. Dan Leary, Director of Administration said, "Our goal is to try to keep accounts receivable under fifty days. We chart accounts receivable that are over sixty days." As a result, since Solid State Circuits introduced charting of accounts receivable, accounts that were past due have steadily dropped to around nine percent.

This particular measurement is the type of assessment that is needed by white collar and service occupations because it is directly under the control of the monitoring group. As one accountant said, "If a guy is late, we call him and say 'you've got to get your money in.'" It is a measure that is especially relevant to accounting and directly impacts quality and productivity. Dan Leary notes, "If we don't have money, we have to borrow it, and borrowing costs us. We can't issue checks on time, which means we're late to our vendors and that puts our credit on hold." He also pointed out that in some cases the company may be able to obtain supplies and products cheaper if they pay on time or sooner. They cannot obtain these discounts if they do not have the cash available.

Is It Worth It?

Is the assessment process worth it? Dan Leary believes it is. He said it lets everyone know what they are supposed to be doing and if they are doing any good. He also said half-kiddingly but with an air of pride, "I knew we were good but I didn't have any proof. Now I do. It gives you instant results on what you're doing. For instance, our manual check writing has gone from 24 to 8 since we began charting it." He also mentioned that accounts receivable was a problem because they did not have anyone working full time, but when they hired a full time person and developed a schedule for calling customers, the results improved dramatically. He also made the point that for managers, assessment and charting gives one a tool for discussion with superiors. There is proof of what has been done for the company. They can point to improvements in critical areas.

Another advantage of assessing and then graphically plotting the results was identified by the President of Solid State Circuits. He said, "It involves everyone assuming more responsibility. Before, inspectors would gather data and then write up negative reports saying personnel were not doing their jobs. Today more and more personnel are gathering and measuring data on their jobs. *Today people are in control of their own destinies.*"

Their assessment and charting process has also produced a better appreciation among departments and within the company of other job responsibilities. As one manager said, "For the first time some people have recognized that others have to meet deadlines. They have learned to appreciate and cooperate with others within the company. That alone is worth it."

COMPONENTS OF ASSESSMENT

Ciba-Geigy, one of the nation's leading producers of agricultural chemicals, decided to find out what their customers thought about their distribution system. They were unsatisfied with typical mail-out surveys, so they used a three-pronged approach that involved mail surveys, telephone interviews, and in-person interviews. The survey results were used to improve operational and communication problems. In 1980 when they started the assessment process, customers rated them as average. By 1984 the assessment process and changes they made because of what they learned resulted in the majority of their customers rating them number one in their field [3]. The key to any assessment is to understand what you want to measure and then act upon the results.

Every organization and manager wanting to improve services must decide how many and which assessment measures to use. The advice here, as in Ciba-Geigy's case, is to use many different kinds. Managers must also decide what criteria will be evaluated, regardless of the method of assessment that is chosen. They will probably want to evaluate the human side of service and the procedural or systems side. Frequently an organization will be good at providing one aspect but not good at the other. Sometimes their human resources service criteria look good while the tasks that require planning and organizing need improvement. Sometimes the opposite is true. Organizations can have procedures and systems set up to provide quality service but it might be that their people do not use the tools that are available. It is very unusual for an organization to be strong in both; many are weak in both. It is those that excel in both areas that produce the exceptional service providers.

Some of the systems or *procedural* aspects that need to be evaluated if organizations are to improve service involve those that address consumer needs. For instance, are procedures in place for resolving customer complaints? Are there organizational procedures that create poor service, such as extensive paperwork or poor return policies? Certainly procedures should be established to properly greet and assist customers. To do this it is necessary to set up procedures to train personnel in the proper methods as well as procedures for evaluating the quality of service provided by them. Organizational concerns will also need to be addressed. For instance, is work properly scheduled so it is possible to provide professional service? Are front-line service providers' work areas properly organized? Are tools and equipment available that enhance and provide timely service?

There are several issues on the human side that also affect service. Any assessment process must include assessment of supervision and personnel. Are your supervisors good coaches that help, rather than hinder, personnel? Are your front-line providers familiar with work they are supposed to do? Unfortunately, today it is rare for a service provider to be highly knowledgeable about the service provided. When is the last time you went in a store and felt that the clerk or reservationist really knew what they were talking about? With little training, incentive, and knowledge of their service, many personnel simply seem to be taking up space rather than making a significant contribution.

You will want to evaluate your personnel at different times of the day. It would be wise to find out if personnel are being attentive despite being rushed. Personnel should project the right appearance. What image is being projected?

In general, service providers need to be pleasant, friendly, helpful. How many times have you seen personnel display disagreeable habits or moods? How many times do they use inappropriate language? What is the body language and attitude of service providers? Is chewing gum inappropriate in some situations? What message does slouching convey?

The link between systems and people is communication. Most good service providers also have a good communication process. They have the people and procedures to insure that customer suggestions and requests are communicated down as well as up through the organization. It should be easy for personnel within the organization to communicate their service problems and suggestions. All too often organizational suggestion boxes and procedures serve little purpose. When suggestions are not acted upon then something is wrong with the system, not the people. People who do their jobs day in and day out are the experts. Under the right situation they can show management how to improve services. It is up to management to provide the conduit for this communication.

KEY POINTS

The customer service provided by white collar and service occupations can be assessed and improved. Displaying job performance and sharing results are ways to improve customer service and profits. As seen, once service measurements are introduced, there are often dramatic improvements in performance.

Often, assessing service, regardless of the methods, helps focus attention on problem areas. As in the Solid State case personnel knew clearly what was expected and quite often that was enough to produce service improvements. There were even indications that charting measurements helped individual and departmental accountability and responsibility. Surprisingly, this also seemed to improve the cooperation and understanding within the organization. Visible measures help people appreciate the interdependence of departments.

To enhance the probability of success one manager emphasized, "Keep at it. Start measuring and assessing service but if it doesn't work out, don't give up—try to think of something else. Try to measure and assess something that's causing headaches on the job or with the customer." Managers need to sit down and look at what causes problems on the job. Identify what you yourself are doing and what others are doing, then establish service measures and investigate causes. When measures stabilize it is time to assess something else. Although almost any assessment is an improvement over none at all, the best ones focus on those criteria a manager can control. As one manager notes, "Assess those things you have control over." This way, responsibility and accountability can be improved.

When assessing service make sure to analyze the subjectivity of those doing the evaluations. It is very important to validate each of the evaluations so that there is agreement on performance. At the heart of this process is to specifically define the objectives of the service measurement and assessment study. This process involves clearly defining an organization's standards for quality performance. Furthermore, those using measurement and assessment tools should clearly understand their use. As we will discuss later, proper training and indoctrination of those using the assessment tools will be vital to their successful implementation. As Ciba-Geigy did, whenever possible use several measurement systems to help insure accurate and reliable information.

An important part of a manager's job will be to sell the system to those who will be involved in the assessment process. Perceptions of those utilizing the system will need to be closely monitored through continual observation. Finally, performance appraisals will be needed to make sure the system is accomplishing its intended purpose. Most of the manager's duties and time will be simplified if the measurement and assessment system can be computerized. This helps assure that the data is efficiently analyzed and also reduces much of the mundane number-crunching of service assessment programs.

The best advice for anyone contemplating using an assessment system would be to evaluate and improve it in the following ways:

- Before conducting an assessment, identify, then define, what services are important to the customer.
- Measure outcomes of services, including the relevant organizational, procedural, and personnel aspects of service.
- Use as many assessment tools as possible to better identify customer needs.
- Try (although it is difficult) to eliminate or at least reduce the subjectivity of the assessment system.
- Make sure everyone knows the system and understands it. If possible get everyone involved in the process, encourage change, use peer pressure positively, and avoid punishment if the change fails to produce the precise results anticipated.
- Assess and chart those things directly under your control.
- Clearly define standards of performance (see next chapter).
- When possible, post results of assessment so everyone can see them.

REFERENCES

1. Rasmussen, MaryAnn E., "Ensuring Quality on a Worldwide Basis," *American Productivity Center Quality Forum*, July 14, 1987, pp. 6–9.
2. Uttal, Bro, "Corporations That Serve You Best," *Fortune*, Dec. 7, 1987, pp. 98–116.
3. Harrington, Lisa H., "What Do Customers Really Want?", *Traffic Management*, August 1985, pp. 50–54.

8

Standards

The purpose of this chapter is to provide a framework for service providers to organize ways of identifying problems and developing solutions in customer service. Each step is a step toward better customer service and long term success. Almost without exception, quality service providers develop and apply standards to their business.

DEFINING SERVICE

The first step in becoming an exceptional service provider is to specifically define exceptional service. Surprisingly, most service organizations or those that provide services often do not do this basic first step. Even if they define service, the definition often does not filter down to employees. For instance, Y. K. Shetty reported in the February 1987 issue of *Management Solutions* that a study of 307 service organizations in southern Florida found that most employees could not define the concept of quality service. Concern for quality was evident in policy statements and quality improvement but it had not reached the employee level [1].

To be successful at providing quality service it is necessary to at least meet and maybe exceed customer expectations. When American Express began its quality assurance efforts in the late 1970s the company began by establishing a quality assurance methodology. The first objective was to, "define their service from the customer's point of view—not from the point of view of a clerk, analyst, manager, director or vice president." Then they wanted to measure service with the same rigor and objectivity that they used in measuring productivity, costs, and revenues [2].

As an illustration of this point, American Express determined that it cost them $2.70 every day their card was unavailable for use by an individual.

Having quantified the cost, the company surveyed customers to determine *their* standards for card issuing. For instance, one task force discovered it took 35 days, on average, to process a charge card application. A survey suggested that applicants became impatient after three weeks; that interval became the new standard of quality [3].

To set standards that meet or exceed customer expectations you must do what American Express did; you must assess customer expectations (Chapter 7). Every business has to sit down and decide exactly what and how much customers expect. As we noted earlier, American Express assesses their customer expectations based on cultural, societal, competitive, and economic, as well as legislative, considerations.

Customer expectations are based on a wide variety of variables. Some questions to answer would be whether or not customers use the service in times of crisis. If they do, their moods and expectations are likely to be different than in normal times. Are customers normally in a good or bad mood when they want to use the services? Any exceptional service provider would identify the likely frame of mind of their customers before they decide what kind of service will be offered.

Research along the lines of customer expectations was conducted for Metropolitan Life by Texas A&M University professors Parasuraman, Zeithaml, and Berry. Their research was able to identify the "most significant factors influencing the overall evaluation." These included an organization's ability to display reliability, responsiveness, tangibles, assurance, and empathy. Reliability refers to the ability to perform the promised service dependably and accurately. Responsiveness involves a willingness to help customers and provide prompt service. Tangibles refers to the physical facilities, equipment, and appearance of personnel. Assurance involves knowledge and courtesy of employees and their ability to convey trust and confidence. Empathy refers to the individual attention and care shown to customers [4].

This research provides one example of what customers at one particular type of business thought was important. Every industry and many within each industry will have their own unique customer expectations. However, it is not enough to simply identify customer expectations. It is also necessary to make sure the organization can deliver what customers expect. That depends a great deal on the type of people within the organization.

Before standards can be defined, it is necessary to assess employee skills, ability, and attitudes. If they do not have the necessary skills to meet proposed standards then either the standards will have to be lowered or training will have to be implemented. If they have the skills but lack motivation, once again, either standards must be changed or incentives provided to enhance motivation. Perhaps more basic is the temperament and personality of front-line service providers. It is not so much a problem for low-contact people, but it is critical for high-customer-contact people. What traits do they need to exhibit? Will they be willing and have the energy to provide the extra touch common to good service?

CRITERIA FOR ESTABLISHING STANDARDS

When standards are established it is important to make sure everyone directly and indirectly involved in delivering the service understands what is expected. Service standards should evaluate two broad but separate criteria. As referred to in the previous chapter, one of those two involves the planning and *organizational* aspects of service. The other involves the personnel side. Each is needed to insure balanced and effective service standards.

Planning and organization considerations include those policies, procedures, methods, and rules that help keep a service system running smoothly. The purpose of these standards is to make the organization as efficient as possible at delivering its services. A systems standard might be one that an efficient service would use to insure responsiveness. For example, Amica Mutual Insurance, considered by some to be an effective service provider, has a performance standard that says, "All customer mail will be answered within one day of receipt of that mail." Such procedures are necessary if an organization is to develop the image of an efficient service provider, but systems alone are not enough.

Human, as well as system, standards must also be set to ensure effective, rather than just efficient, service. Personnel considerations include those attributes of front-line service providers that help establish relationships with customers. Customers deal with people, not corporations. They feel comfortable when they know the personnel and when personnel know something about them.

Relationships are certainly important but they cannot stand alone. If a good delivery or training system is not in place, customers will end up not getting what they want when they want it. If this situation continues to occur, no amount of friendly and personable front-line service will be able to build customer loyalty.

Systems Considerations

As we noted earlier, every organization will need to decide what criteria are important to their customers. However, some of the more common types of customer concerns can be reviewed here. Services need to be well organized so that what is intended will be provided. Employees, equipment, and material supplies need to be scheduled so there is a smooth flow and customers suffer as few inconveniences as possible. Domino's, L.L. Bean, Southland Corporation, American Airlines, and other service providers all have their rush, or peak, times. They would not be able to provide quality service if they had not planned and prepared for those times. A smoothly organized flow of services occurring at regular intervals should be an objective, but there are always irregular demand patterns. Good scheduling of resources, monitoring flow of services, and flexibility in responding to changes are critical. Byerly's and other top service providers, for example, have systems set up so customers rarely have to wait more than a few minutes in line.

As indicated by earlier research, customers also tend to want services that are responsive and convenient. System procedures should be set up for the convenience of the customer, not the business. Often, convenience for the customer refers to how long it takes to receive the service. American Express adjusting their standards and process of applying for credit cards to suit the customers' expectations is an example of this responsiveness.

In other cases, convenience is defined by the length of wait: in line, on the telephone, and so forth. Top service providers know their customers and know what they expect. They know when customers are likely to renege or when they are likely to simply balk and refuse to join the line. The length of time customers are willing to wait varies from doctors' offices to service stations to ski resorts. As in American Express' case, an organization needs to find out these answers and only then can reasonable standards be set. Domino's Pizza's "30 minutes or it's free" is an example of a standard that is based on what the organization is capable of doing and what the customer expects.

True service occurs when it is given before the customer asks for it. When people have to ask for help, a service opportunity has already been missed. The best service is preventive rather than reactive. To accomplish this, frontline service providers and their managers must know both the sequence and order of customer activities that are going to occur. This is critical to developing the customer's perspective so essential to good service.

Timing is critical in sports, and in business as well. Set up systems so personnel know what is going to happen before it happens. One such standard might state, "Personnel are to immediately acknowledge guests upon their arrival at the establishment." Another timing standard might be set up to offer assistance or to anticipate a customer's needs. A typical example involves telephone customers where operators are instructed to come back on the line after a person is on hold every 30 seconds to see if they wish to continue to hold or "leave a message."

Any service standards that do not address *communication* concerns are likely to be unrealistic. Obviously there must be good communication about the service between service personnel and their customers. A typical standard in this area might require personnel, at appropriate times, to inquire about the customer's satisfaction with their service.

Communication is also essential between service personnel and their managers. Any weakness within, or up and down in the organization will create ineffective service. Systems will need to be set up, communication training will need to occur, incentives will need to be established, and the process will need checkpoints so it can be evaluated. This will also entail establishing a means for customers to communicate their concerns.

This is similar to the process that American Express went through when they began their quality assurance process. They realized they were measuring performance in the wrong way. They had been measuring the work of individual departments. While individual departments were generally doing OK, their overall process needed improvement. They noted that, "customers perceive quality in terms of the whole not just in parts." With this realization American Express began what they called their "enlightenment phase." Rather than measure individual departments, they adopted a customer-perspective way of thinking and measuring. They began to "break down the walls between departments." They began tracking the flow of consumer services from one end of the organization to the other and from one geographic region to the next. Then they divided their transactions where they were visible and measurable to their customers, such as processing new accounts, billing card members, paying service establishments, handling inquiries, and replacing lost or stolen cards [2]. It was a systematic rather than bureaucratic approach that focused on measurable activities, not disconnected departments. Once this was done, meaningful standards were easier to establish.

Human Considerations

Responsive and dependable customer service comes from systematic application of standards. However, customers often want more than fast and consistent service. Someone can be fast but show no courtesy or kindness. They can be available but show little empathy. Compared to system considerations, human considerations are of equal or greater importance. Rapport and trust with customers are invaluable for almost any organization, and only people can give that. As noted previously, a manager at Nordstrom said they like to hire "nice people." Managers in every organization must decide for themselves what human traits they wish to emphasize, but a few of the more common positive human service traits can be mentioned.

Most customers appreciate personal attention. Although not always possible, most customers appreciate it when service personnel show attention or refer to them by their first name. It shows that personnel have taken the time and effort to get to know, at least in name, the customer. It communicates respect and makes service seem less bureaucratic.

Nordstrom, the high-service Seattle based retailer, makes a great impression with their "Personal Touch" program. It is a complimentary service that helps customers choose clothing, shoes, and accessories that match each individual's style and taste. The store assigns a Personal Touch consultant to a customer. The consultant, not the customer, searches the store for items they think a customer might like and then brings the items to the customer to try on. They also advise the customer on selecting certain styles and colors of merchandise. The items can even be chosen by a personal consultant so they are available to try on when a customer arrives at the store.

Although it may not always be possible to provide such personal service or to know customers on a first name basis, it is always wise to present a respectful and friendly image. The best service providers have a genuine concern for their customers. Standards should encourage service providers to try to give the personal touch so customers do not just feel like they are a number waiting to be processed. A typical standard for greeting customers might be, "Each customer will be acknowledged within 20 seconds of entering the building by using the customer's first name." Another standard might be, "In conversation a customer's name must be used at least once."

Setting standards for proper behavior is important, but some aspects of service will remain intangible. That is why it is important to recruit "service people." Many of our service organizations would agree with the manager of Texas Instruments' CRC. She said that to provide good service you have to have people who want to serve. Some people are good high-contact people, others are not.

Service is nonverbal as well as verbal. Sometimes it is not so much the answer to questions as much as how the answer is given that is critical to a customer's impression. As much as possible, standards should refer to the need to make eye contact and to be aware of facial and body expressions. Do service providers convey a positive helping message or something else? Most of us know when someone does not want to be bothered. It can be seen in an abrupt attitude. It can be seen in the way a service person stands. Some clearly demonstrate that they are interested in helping, while others just go through the motions. Standards and training need to be established so the right tone is set.

Standards need to be developed for the human as well as system side. Service personnel not only need to know the right answers, they also need to be trained and evaluated based on how the answer was presented. Were they tactful or rude? Were they pleasant or offensive? Was there sincerity or sarcasm?

Standards should be established for display of positive attitudes. Service providers should be expected to volunteer helpful suggestions rather than the customer prying them out. Service providers should be decisive, they should be knowledgeable about their product or service. How many times have you heard a service person say, "I don't know" or "You'll have to see the manager"?

As can be seen, setting standards takes time and a lot of thought, but it is time well spent. Standards, along with effective training and incentives to provide good service, are critical to establishing a system of high quality service.

ESTABLISHING STANDARDS

Once a business has considered as many variables as possible it can then establish standards for a wide array of service conditions. The purpose of and mechanics for establishing standards are fairly simple and straightforward. Standards provide a clear definition and expectation for management, employees, and customers. Customers know what to expect and generally get it. Employees know how they will be judged, and supervision is less arbitrary and subjective.

Most capable and competent people want realistic and easily understood goals. Measurable standards make it easier to assess performance and give fair, equitable incentives for service.

The actual process of developing and setting standards consists of three parts. The first part is the *purpose*. Before any standards are established, management should determine why they need to be developed. Management must decide what kind of service behavior they are trying to create. They must decide what message they want to send the customer. Every standard sends a message. Management should understand what is being communicated to the customer. If standards promise a satisfaction guarantee and if time or quality standards must be met, then it sends a positive message to customers. On the other hand, if a business offers service "in about an hour" but has no standards and no reaction when standards are not met, then the service message is decidedly negative.

Standards, in addition to needing a purpose, must also *describe what is expected*, such as "employees will greet all customers within two minutes of their arrival." This action phrase shows that whoever developed this standard can clearly identify what is expected. Some action phrases often seen in service standards include things such as "greet" or "respond to the customer by saying . . ." or "it must be delivered within . . ." It is important for management to plan what type of behavior is to be exhibited and then clearly spell it out in the standard. A typical standard with an action phrase would be, "Management will open up an additional check-out line when the line at any station exceeds 3 customers in length."

The third and final part of standard setting involves the need to *make the service measurable*. When Raymond J. Larkin, American Express TRS's Vice President of Operations, was discussing how they had achieved such quality assurance results, he said their ultimate objective "was to make a science out of service and to make customer service requirements quantifiable" [5]. In fact, without numbers it is extremely difficult to determine if standards are being met. As we noted in the introduction, "If you can't measure it, you can't improve it."

Many of the top service providers try to make a point of measuring the service levels delivered to their customers. For example, American Airlines has a requirement that no more than 85% of their passengers should have to wait in line for more than five minutes to buy a ticket. Their service standards also include answering reservation phones within 20 seconds, opening airplane doors in less than 70 seconds after the plane pulls up to the gate, and having 85% of their flights land within 15 minutes of scheduled arrival time. These standards are then used to determine staffing levels [6].

These American Airlines measurements are time-based standards. It is also possible to measure service that has occurred through counting written or real transactions. For instance, one could count the number of homes shown, or new listings of homes secured, and incorporate the numbers in a log book. Other measures could be based on some physical quantity, quality, size, or other relevant service standard.

In some cases it is wise to even identify the specific words and phrases service providers should use when interacting with customers such as, "Good morning, how can I help you?" These phrases or words could refer to a description of the service available or simply be a professional and friendly greeting.

The objective of these scripts is to give the customer both the right information and right image. For instance, "Good morning, today we are offering . . ." Of course it will require practice and concentration to avoid appearing "canned" or "mechanical." Some organizations prefer to be more flexible, and instead, have general guidelines on what should be said.

Regardless of whether there is a script or not, it will be important to establish nonverbal standards. Smiles, eye-contact, and warm welcoming attitudes are important. Sloppy posture, chewing gum, or disinterested looks are usually things high-contact service people should avoid. They can ruin the best prepared script and system available for quality service.

The need to decentralize services is a matter of great importance to effective services. We will discuss this later but one point can be made here. If possible, it is obviously wise to involve personnel in the creation of their own standards, much like SRC does. No one knows the demands and conditions of their jobs better than those who provide the services.

If personnel are allowed to establish their own standards, commitment to those standards is built in. SRC, as well as some others, sit down with their employees, decide together what is needed, what can be done, and how much money will be needed to achieve the desired results. Such a process recognizes the service provider as a worthwhile key to quality service.

Meaningful commitment to service standards can never be completely passed down, it must be built up.

The final comment about establishing standards involves their dynamic nature. Service standards should not be established and forgotten. A business environment is constantly changing and so are the conditions that created the standards. Performance to standards needs to be evaluated and corrected if necessary. Often the conditions of employment change and the standards themselves have to be modified. Assessing these changes should be based on customer expectations and feedback, competition, and social changes.

MEASURING AND MONITORING PERFORMANCE

Standards identify what should be done but not necessarily what is done. Researchers at Texas A&M noted that, "What we've learned is that quality of service is measured by the difference between the expectation of the customer on the one hand, and the customer's perceived level of service delivered on the other. The gap between the two points represents the size of the service problem" [7].

Assuming service standards are based on customer expectations, as in the case of American Express, the next challenge is to track those expectations. American Express does this through "transaction based" surveys that measure the quality of specific customer transactions such as telephone inquiries, billing questions, and authorization processing at the time of purchase [5]. These surveys are then analyzed so that corrective action can be taken if necessary.

They also use an on-site business review as a means of monitoring performance. Corporate officers visit their various centers throughout the world. They review and assess quality, competition, marketing, and operational systems at the various centers. Often such visits may last several weeks. In the end the reviewers point out steps needed to improve quality service. Their standards are high. As already noted, anyone who has a department whose performance falls below 98% must explain, to the quality assurance staff's satisfaction, why standards are not being met. Some of the performance measures that they use include: average number of days from receipt of applications to mailing of credit card or decline notification; percentage of replacement cards available on the same day as the emergency request for replacement; percent of address changes which are processed correctly, and so forth.

Making use of personal observations as American Express and the other service providers do is probably the most common and simplest way of checking on performance to standards. The posture of these observations should be to assume a questioning attitude, rather than fault-finding. The purpose of such observations is to look for examples of both satisfactory and unsatisfactory adherence to service standards. It is what MaryAnne Rasmussen, American Express TRS's Vice President of Worldwide Quality Assurance calls, "Management by walking around, listening . . . and immediately calling service improvement opportunities to the attention of employees" [5].

Written or oral reports are also a popular way of evaluating performance to standards. The medium may vary from one service provider to the next but the idea is to have clear, concise reports that identify strengths, weaknesses, and opportunities. American Express, American Airlines, SRC, and a variety of other top service providers use these reports to monitor and statistically track performance on many key measures.

An example of such an effective written evaluation system is demonstrated by Northern Telecom, Inc. This organization is an international corporation manufacturing telecommunication equipment. Their headquarters is located in Nashville, Tennessee.

In 1980 they began a Customer Satisfaction Program that was designed to establish a uniform method of measuring key elements of quality. Their procedure was designed to track customer satisfaction and identify areas of customer dissatisfaction so steps could be taken to correct root causes of problems.

Their written customer satisfaction tracking system consists of three specific questionnaires. The first is mailed to customers about 30 days after the installation of a product. It focuses on sales, marketing services, delivery, installation, and training. The second questionnaire is mailed six months after customer installation and its format focuses on product performance, maintenance service, and repair service. The third and final questionnaire is mailed at one-year intervals throughout the entire ownership period and focuses on variables that relate to product use. Each of the instruments contain satisfaction and repurchase measures which form the basis for indexing performance. Northern Telecom's customer satisfaction system is able to provide the headquarters Quality Assurance Department and division managers with information about specific concerns and gives them an effective and objective way of appraising strengths and weaknesses [8].

CORRECTIVE ACTION AND WORK IMPROVEMENTS

Corrective action will only be needed if there is a deviation between what was expected (e.g., service standards) and what actually happened. For instance, if a standard calls for delivery of services or products in "30 minutes or less" and it takes 40 minutes, then corrective measures will be needed, providing the deviation was not expected.

This type of corrective approach is often referred to in management literature as "management-by-exception." In management-by-exception, managers focus on unusual or exceptional deviations from standards, rather than every deviation, thus prioritizing time and efforts. Management can then focus attention on the most critical service needs. The key point is to determine whether a deviation is exceptional. This focuses efforts of management on exceptional rather than routine service problems. Of course, management-by-exception should be used for good as well as poor performance. Unusual performance, any unusual performance, should be investigated.

This style of management also provides an effective way to delegate to front-line service providers, thus pushing responsibilities further down the chain of command. For instance, routine customer problems and complaints can be handled by front-line employees; only unusual problems or requests would be handled by management. If failure to meet a standard that called for delivery of a product in 30 minutes or less was caused by some routine problem like bad weather, then the problem can be handled by the service providers. However, if the cause of the deviation was unexpected, then management will need to assess the root cause. If the delivery could not be made and its delivery was within normal parameters (weather, territory, preparation time, delivery time, etc.) then management must discover and correct the root causes.

Before taking action, remember that there are four reasons why these deviations might occur. First and foremost, management must decide if the service standards are reasonable. In some cases it may be next to impossible to deliver appropriate services in 30 minutes. If the standards are unlikely to be achieved then they should be changed, or the conditions changed, so it is possible.

Secondly, there may be a deviation between what was expected and what occurred because personnel could not do the job since they were not properly trained. If front-line service providers or their supervisors are not qualified to do the job (e.g., do not know how to deliver the service), then management cannot expect performance standards to be met.

Thirdly, it is possible because of the interdependent nature of service that the preceding task contributed to creating the problem. For instance, if someone was late delivering a service, it is possible that they in turn were notified too late about the customer's order. Standards were violated but it was not the service provider's fault.

Finally, there is the possibility that it was in fact the service provider's fault. If it is due to employee neglect or a personnel problem, then a variety of management actions can occur. It is possible to retrain and motivate service providers who do not meet standards. Personnel can be shifted from one position to another so standards can be met. Counseling, reprimands, and even termination are other ways of dealing with those who do not meet reasonable performance standards.

KEY POINTS

Setting standards, measuring performance to those standards, making corrections, and taking action do improve the quality of service. American Express' Raymond J. Larkin noted that measuring service "had profound effects on the way we did business. We changed workflows, eliminated unnecessary steps . . . examined root causes, eliminated problems . . . restructured organizations and changed reporting lines because our primary focus was on the customer" [2]. The process of measuring performance and taking corrective action when needed helped American Express come up with new methods, procedures, and ideas for improving service and profits. It was one of the key reasons why, in three years, the company was able to improve quality service delivery by 78%, reduce expenses per customer transaction by 21%, and reduce application processing time by 37%. Such combined improvements are an example of qualitivity. Larkin notes that their quality assurance process has added hundreds of millions of dollars to American Express' bottom line [2]. Key ingredients to implementing performance standards include:

- Specifically define what exceptional service is
- Assess and establish standards so you are able to meet customer expectations
- Define service from the customer's point of view by identifying factors affecting the customer's evaluation of the service
- Specifically define the systems and human characteristics (verbal and non-verbal) and attitudes needed to deliver quality service
- Before setting standards, define the purpose and action expected from implementing standards
- Encourage front-line service personnel to become involved in standard-setting
- Make standards measurable and quantifiable
- Measure and monitor adherence to performance standards through written and personal observations
- Identify root causes and take corrective action when there is a difference between what is expected and what was achieved

REFERENCES

1. Shetty, Y. K., "Guidelines for Managing In Service Business," *Management Solutions*, February 1987, p. 38.
2. Larkin, Raymond J., "The History of Quality At American Express," *American Productivity Center Quality Forum*, July 14, 1987, pp. 1–5.
3. Haskett, James L., *Managing in the Service Economy*, Boston, Mass., Harvard Business School Press, 1986, p. 96.
4. "Viewing Service Quality at Metropolitan Life," *The Quality Review*, Winter 1987, p. 14.
5. Blickstein, Steve, "It's in the Cards," *The Quality Review*, Winter 1987, p. 6.
6. Main, Jeremy, "Toward Service Without A Snare," *Fortune*, March 23, 1981, p. 64.
7. "Quality: The Competitive Advantage," (Paid Advertising Section), *Fortune*, September 28, 1987.
8. U.S. Office of Consumer Affairs, *Consumer Complaint Handling in America: AN UPDATE STUDY PART II*, April 1, 1986 (Washington: Government Printing Office), pp. 11–12.

9

Training For Services

If services are to be improved it is abundantly clear from research and successful service organizations that front-line personnel and their managers must understand how to deliver services, and want to deliver them. As we already discussed in several chapters, service providers like Texas Instruments CRC, Holiday Inn, Walt Disney, and others provide extensive training for their personnel. Of course, most organizations provide some employee training. In service, as in many areas, it is not so much a matter of doing as the degree to which it's done. Everyone trains, but some really train correctly.

Because training is generally much more extensive in manufacturing than in services the best examples of effective training often come from manufacturing settings. Moreover, it is often the Japanese manufacturer that places great value on extensive training. An example of this is Nissan.

The Nissan plant in Smyrna, Tennessee is an example of a place where training is taken seriously. There is the usual technical training for employees; anywhere from 16 to 360 hours of pre-employment training in skills such as welding, painting, or forklift operations. It is, however, Nissan's commitment that separates them from most. When they began operations, 380 of their supervisory personnel and technicians were sent to Japan for training and practical experience. Technicians spent six weeks, while supervisors spent about 40 weeks in training in Japan. The bottom line was that Nissan spent $63 million in initial truck training. An additional $10.4 million was spent in training for the second shift. Now that is real commitment.

Today training continues to be emphasized. Technicians are encouraged to learn as many jobs as possible. Extensive on-the-job training and a pay-for-versatility program rewards technicians who acquire versatility. They have built a four-million-dollar training center that is equipped with almost every piece of equipment found within the plant, so employees can learn at their own pace. At the training center there are courses other than those of a technical nature. Courses in problem solving, interpersonal skills, conducting effective meetings, and listening skills are some of the subjects that every employee takes.

Manufacturers are not the only ones with extensive training programs. In a recent issue of *Fortune* magazine [1], Merck, a drug maker, was ranked number one for service to pharmacists and doctors. Their success is in part due to their comprehensive training programs for their salespeople. New employees study basic medical subjects for ten weeks and must score 90% or better on a weekly test to stay in the program. After this training they enter phase two, where they spend an additional three weeks learning how to present Merck products. They then make presentations in the field along with their district manager for six months. Phase three training consists of three weeks at the headquarters improving presentation skills.

TRAINING FOR POTENTIAL

Most training programs either prepare employees to do a specific task or orient them to a particular area, but the best ones try to maximize an employee's potential. As already noted in chapter two, this training is an ongoing process at Springfield Remanufacturing Corporation (SRC). A great deal of their corporate success is based on their process of training and their philosophy toward training.

Mike Carrigan, vice president at SRC, says that he has seen the difference the training and education program has made. He said management tends to be made up of difficult or easy tasks. He believes that most managers find it difficult, for example, to apply punishment or discipline.

Often even encouraging and simply telling people they are doing a good job can be a difficult task. Adhering to production schedules, as well as issuing reprimands and providing positive encouragement, would also be difficult for many managers.

Carrigan emphasized the effects of their training and education philosophy when he said, "One or one and one-half years ago either I or my middle managers did all difficult tasks. If a first-line manager had to do one of these difficult tasks they went all to pieces. Today less than 30% of these difficult tasks are done by upper management and over 70% of these tasks are performed by floor managers."

Carrigan said that one of the best benefits for himself and the organization has been quicker decision making, primarily because decision making occurs at a much lower level. In addition, he believes it has motivated others to do their job better. Gary Brown, SRC's Human Resource Director, echoed these feelings when he said that when a manager does one of these challenging managerial tasks, they are proud of it. He said, "Their self-confidence and control have increased dramatically."

The training and education program has also produced better executive time management for them. Mike Carrigan mentioned that at one time he spent 50% of his time on the production floor dealing with supervisory-level problems. Today, he spends less than 15% of his time on the production floor. Now he has more time to devote to decisions which only he can make. SRC has always had a participatory style so floor personnel have known that they had the necessary authority and responsibility. Today though, thanks in part to their training philosophy, SRC's personnel increasingly know how to handle that authority and responsibility.

They have training programs for all levels of management. This includes training for their personnel in key positions: engineers, accountants, sales, and so forth. They also have the typical training for "executive development" that includes people who are a step higher on the organizational ladder: those in middle and upper management positions. And as with any good training program, SRC also trains their hourly personnel. However, this is not what makes their training program unique. What is unique is their focus or philosophy behind the programs; the real key to their success.

INTELLIGENT PHILOSOPHY

It is management's responsibility to teach all personnel a basic understanding of how an organization works. Jack Stack, the president of SRC, bases his philosophy on the knowledge that better informed employees make more productive and committed members of the team. He believes in developing the employee's basic understanding of a wide range of financial and business concepts. He teaches them the "rules of the game." He shows how each employee contributes to the profit and loss column.

Behind the action is the belief that all of their employees are intelligent. Stack and his management team believe it is their objective to tap this intelligence so personnel can become productive. They believe their employees have an innate ability to comprehend and understand the meaning of business. They believe front-line employees have an ability to adapt to new situations, and to reason and think intelligently. Given understanding and background, they know their front-line can grasp ideas and relations and then exercise dispassionate reasoning. This reasoned, clear-headed, and well-informed thinking is the very heart of what we mean by *intelligence*. An example of how this philosophy is implemented can be seen in SRC's approach to financial training. All the hourly employees are taught financial concepts such as reading financial statements and balance sheets by the president and other upper management officers.

Other training is built into the job personnel must do. As previously mentioned first-line managers are given responsibility to monitor and control organization-wide commodities like abrasives and chemicals. These overhead items become the exclusive domain of that person.

Such corporate-wide perspectives teach personnel about new areas and help them gain an organization-wide perspective and develop a teamwork attitude. This approach keeps everyone better-informed and thereby more likely to listen to reason. By its nature the approach also requires personnel to be more inventive and more creative.

Other than promoting better management, what has been the result of such a unique training philosophy? For one thing, SRC's prime labor utilization has been exceptional. Their recent goal was 88% utilization; thus only 12% of the time would their direct or prime labor be involved in nonproductive activities. Nonproductive activities include such things as absenteeism, rework, vacations, and so on. Direct time refers to the time where employees were directly involved in performing their assigned tasks. SRC exceeded this 88% goal; their personnel had 90% prime labor utilization.

INTELLIGENT TRAINING

Many managers today seem to limit the ability and maybe even intelligence of their employees when they "expect" incompetence or expect the worst. Perceptions do change things. There are self-fulfilling prophecies. Productive managers know this, see the best, and act accordingly.

Upper management at SRC expects productive and intelligent attitudes from its people and will not have it any other way. Employees have a positive attitude partly because they are treated as equals. One vice president at SRC emphasized this when he said, "We set a corporate program of open communication. We share everything. If we have something to share we go out and do it. It sets a corporate strategy that we must communicate if we are going to survive. If everyone feels they have a right and obligation to communicate, it makes them grow. You become more precise in what you prepare to communicate." The organization's approach to openly communicating and sharing information helps produce knowledgeable and well-informed employees.

If management wants intelligent front-line employees they must also *show them how to play the "game" of business.* We cannot expect workers to act intelligently if they do not understand the rules of the game. To react intelligently employees must understand how everything fits together. At SRC employees understand why decisions are made and what factors are considered before they begin to play the "game" of business. Helping them understand and get involved in the success of the business means the management must first teach them the financial rules of the game. Teaching employees about income statements and balance sheets is a start in teaching them some of the rules of the game. It is also a way of ensuring intelligent front-line service providers and first rate service.

A PERSPECTIVE ON TRAINING

The quality of service is largely dependent on how well front-line people are treated when they first come to work, and every day after that. Research shows that front-line service providers tend to treat customers the way they themselves are treated. Organizations with poor service often treat their employees as if they were unimportant and unintelligent. Indifference begets indifference.

SRC provides a good example of the opposite approach. Employees are not treated indifferently or as if they were unintelligent. They are treated as if they are a vital part of the organization. The degree of SRC's trust and respect for the intelligence of their employees is rare among organizations.

Gary Brown, human resources director for SRC, says that prospective and current employees know they must learn the practical considerations of their jobs. When employees are hired they are told that 85% of their compensation is for performing their jobs and 15% is for learning the business aspects of the jobs. While many companies may profess such a philosophy, SRC is one of the few that follows through on this commitment.

Some companies tell their employees what the performance standards will be, and then tell them if the standards are not met the company loses money. They also tell employees that if standards are exceeded the company (and employee) makes money. This approach has varying degrees of success.

SRC goes beyond this approach by *training* the employee to understand and appreciate the company's point of view. Instead of giving employees standards to meet, they let employees actually *set their own standards and budgets* for their own work areas. Usually an engineer, the employee's front-line supervisor, and the employee are involved in setting the standard. Together they determine the employee's and the work area's capabilities. It is management-by-objectives applied at the lowest level within the organization.

While participation in standard setting provides valuable training for employees, it is the participative budget-setting process that truly makes SRC unique. All employees not only actively participate in setting their job standards, but they also participate in establishing their own budget for their work areas. Employees are first asked what level of production they feel they can achieve. Then they are asked how much overhead cost will be involved in meeting their production goals.

In most organizations, upper management gives a supervisor a budget of, for example, $150,000. Then that money is strictly monitored. At SRC, front-line managers decide how much they need to run an area, and then upper management simply keeps that total in focus. They are not worried so much about each line of the budget. For example, if a front-line manager loses a $20,000 a year employee, then he/she could request two $10,000 employees or one $20,000 employee in replacement. If the same supervisor has a 5% raise budgeted for the department, he/she can choose to give one employee a 10% raise and another no raise. As long as the average of 5% is maintained, it is up to the supervisor to decide the distribution.

Gary Brown states, "Essentially, we make a manager out of a blue collar worker." Although SRC monitors employee financial figures and projections, they do not focus on each line item. As long as these overhead costs stay within the proposed budget, it is primarily the employee's responsibility to keep those costs under control.

SRC provides the opportunity for learning and gives employees the responsibility and accountability to make the experience meaningful. It is unlikely that a more comprehensive way to train and educate employees could be found. The company shows employees how they fit within the corporate picture and asks them to assume responsibility and accountability for their jobs.

Contrast this attitude to the attitude of organizations with poor service. Here the "boss" is the only one respected. Disrespect starts just below the top level and flows downward. Each level treats each lower level with less and less respect. Disrespect, rudeness, and impatience are passed on to the customer. It ends in interactions with the customer, but the whole organization pays the price of lost customers.

SELECTION AND ORIENTATION

Quality service begins with the job interview. Hiring the right people is essential. Many effective service providers recognize the importance of the interview process. Disney treats recruitment and selection very seriously. They have a one-hour presentation on corporate values and want people to "back out" if they feel they cannot meet the standards [2]. As will be seen in the chapter on decentralization, one organization believes so much in the importance of selection that it hires a consulting psychologist to help make hiring and promotional decisions. This may be an extreme approach for many, but serious thought must be given to what characteristics and attributes will be needed by an organization's front-line personnel. Certainly communication, problem-solving abilities and empathy are positive service attributes. We want our service providers to exercise good judgement, to be dependable, and have enough desire and energy to want to serve. While these attributes are obviously valuable, it is wise for service management to sit down and determine what specific service attributes are most important to their organization.

Regardless of personality traits, it is essential that employees recognize their own value to the company and the company's corresponding emphasis on service. The best place to begin this process is in employee orientation. First impressions do matter. Many experts believe the orientation process is the key to whether employees become effective service providers or not.

Orientations should teach employees about their responsibilities and show how, where, and why they are accountable for service, make them feel secure and needed, and show them the corporate history and impart the vision and organizational philosophy. L.L. Bean, like so many other successful service providers, always has new employees review a videotape about the company and then introduces them to the company's unique approach toward the customer.

Most orientations describe what is expected of employees. Effective ones also identify how an employee's job relates to service and other organizational goals. In addition to explanations of pay, benefits, and other normal activities, effective orientations also identify opportunities for growth, advancement, and each person's role in providing quality service.

SKILL ENHANCEMENT

Personnel cannot serve, regardless of whether they want to or not, if they do not have the necessary skills to do so. If a service provider is illiterate, then certain directions and reading skills are impossible. Training can be designed to eliminate the problem if it affects customer service, or pictures and other non-reading forms of instructions can be used to help illiterate service providers. Illiteracy is a problem in many service organizations such as restaurants, hotels, food services, and housekeeping services that depend on poorly-educated personnel to provide some of their services.

Depending on the situation, a wide range of skills may be necessary to provide quality service. Skill-based training at American Airlines was based on the corporation's desire for managers to function in a more participatory environment. Therefore, managers were trained in problem-solving skills. American Airlines reasons that it is impossible to participate if one does not know how to solve problems. Managers also received leadership training that de-emphasized autocratic management. Instead, it showed managers how to coach and counsel for performance. Communication and interpersonal skills were also emphasized.

Other skill-based training successfully being used includes stress management. Chris Lee, managing editor of *Training*, reported that the Southern California Gas Company used stress management to both reduce turnover of front-line personnel and increase customer satisfaction [3]. It is stressful to deal with the wide variety of attitudes, temperaments, and dispositions of customers. Some are upset, some want information, others want satisfaction, some are just grumpy, and others just need help.

The company hired a consultant to train their own company trainers on stress reduction techniques. These people would then later train other members. The organization set up role-playing situations, wrote the "scripts" for those real-life situations and acted out those scenes. The scenes were videotaped and used as part of the training process. Personnel were also introduced to human relations and transactional analysis.

The conclusion of one of the trainers is, "It really works to treat customers as you'd like to be treated. You don't think of [a customer interaction] as a confrontation." Stress management techniques do help. Southern California Gas Co. customer service representatives periodically evaluate twenty different consumer areas (e.g., did they solve the customer's problem, etc.), and found, overall, that quality service improved because personnel were better at dealing with customers and their own stress.

Role playing is an effective method of training in service management skills. Larry Robinson wrote in the *Harvard Business Review* that role playing helped his business provide better service [4]. He directs J. B. Robinson Jewelers, Inc., and states that each advancement by employees requires that employees pass tests covering sales ability, product knowledge, and procedures. Each test requires role playing where a store manager, acting as a customer, interacts with the employee. The role play is demonstrated before a panel of judges consisting of the store manager and a supervisor.

His suggestions for successful role playing include designing it to focus on special subjects (e.g., greeting customers, closing a sale, handling complaints, etc.). Second, role playing should challenge personnel by having them interact with a demanding, resistant, or otherwise challenging customer. Debriefing is also wise: having salespeople tell what they felt they could have done better. Comments from others should be sought about good points and areas where the presentation could have been improved. He especially emphasized the need to avoid trying to teach "one best way" because there is not one best way. Service providers should be encouraged to use their flexibility, intuition, and imagination.

TRAINING THE RIGHT ATTITUDE

When most people think of lousy service, what they often are thinking about are "common courtesies" or rather, the lack of them. Too few front-line service providers are trained in the art of providing services. It is amazing that such a fundamental part of service does not exist. As much as customers are affected by first impressions, you would think that business would instruct, monitor, and reward for courtesies given to customers.

Basic courtesies of smiling, saying "thank you," and acting civil are not common occurrences in many businesses. When is the last time someone smiled when you returned something? How many times were you greeted promptly when you entered a business or store? Wal-Mart does it and so do some expensive restaurants, but frequently even these common-sense gestures are often ignored by businesses.

When you think about it, it is truly amazing that an example of courtesy comes from Wal-Mart, a self-service firm. It is the "full service" organizations that have exhibited the greatest drop in service. Often at these facilities the only "thank you" you receive is printed on the receipt. Many times frequent customers at retail stores or banks and other establishments are not welcomed back. Ask yourself how many times did the phone ring before an employee answered it? How was it answered: courteously? Customers sometimes find themselves on hold for what seems an eternity. Contrast this to many of our exceptional service providers that require that a phone is answered before the third ring. If left on hold the operator checks back every thirty seconds or so.

Friendly service will only become better when there is better selection and training of personnel. Service firms should not hire or keep "grumps." Some people look on the positive side and some do not. Services need "people" persons. They need people who like to be with others. Smiling for some is natural, for others it is not. Impatient salespeople or clerks can destroy the best promotional and advertising programs.

Once an organization has selected the traits they want their people to exhibit and have hired the best available personnel, the rest depends on training and motivation. Standards on courtesy will need to be developed and frequently reviewed. Unless employees know the standards and are given feedback on their performance, long term improvement cannot occur. Incentives are also a powerful encouragement.

Courtesies, cooperation, responsibility, or any number of other desirable traits are more likely when management, like SRC's management, has a positive attitude toward their employees, and more likely when those employees have a positive attitude toward themselves. *Self-respect* is important to good service. If personnel feel good about themselves and the way they are treated, they are more likely to give good service.

It is not easy to live up to this attitude of faith in employee judgment, but upper management at SRC proves it in their everyday interactions with employees. For instance, in 1987 when they lost almost 25% of their business because G.M., their principal customer, "downsized" and cancelled all orders, they faced a critical decision. The president was faced with a choice of laying off many people or keeping them and hoping business would pick up. If he laid off several hundred people, then the ones that were left would have secure jobs. On the other hand, if he kept all his employees, he ran the risk of putting everyone in financial danger.

After some thought he decided to let his employees decide what to do. He presented the proposal and risk to them. Overwhelmingly, all the employees decided to not lay off anyone and instead ran the financial risk. They decided to try to go out and obtain more business, to "tighten their belts," reduce overhead, and improve productivity. It worked. Today SRC is stronger financially than before the crisis. In large part it was due to everyone pulling together. They could do this because they not only had the right technical skills but also employees were trained in the right attitude.

Wegman Foods, an effective service provider featured in *Fortune* magazine, also tries to instill a positive attitude in their people through education [1]. Usually grocery stores have a great deal of trouble with turnover and ineffective service. Personnel at Wegman are not so eager to leave because the president of the company offers a college scholarship for employees who perform well, can write a convincing application, and who appear likely to do well in college. Those scholarships are for one-half tuition at a college or graduate school. Today 1,000 of the 11,000 employees are still in college. That is training that motivates. One customer noted, "I've lived in Japan and service at Wegman's is just like service in Japan." The company also has an effective work-study program geared to high school students who might otherwise drop out of school.

In the same article Embassy Suite Hotel's president Hervey Feldman noted that his minimum wage employees, with training and experience, have the curiosity and intelligence to go beyond making beds. He encourages this attitude by hiring and promoting managers who share this attitude. He builds a management support base by hiring and promoting managers with interpersonal skills who treat people as if they were competent. He also encourages employee growth by setting up an incentive program based on pay for skills. For example, a housekeeper can learn new skills and when a new position becomes available, move to a better position such as front desk worker. Approximately one quarter of their employees are usually in training.

Domino's Pizza, as noted in Chapters 5 and 10, also uses a similar type of progressive growth and career training program. While most employees start out as drivers or pizza makers, personnel have the opportunity to keep learning and moving up through the organization. Within a couple of years many are managing their own stores. Many others go on to own their own franchise operations. Employees can see the direct link between training and performance. Most of the upper management at Domino's and most of the franchise owners started out as drivers or pizza makers. Pepsi-Cola General Bottlers uses a similar from-the-ground-up style of promotion, which makes for an operationally sound and service-conscious management.

Of course, this promotion path is not the only way to show that front-line service providers are the "backbone of a business." Regardless of how it is achieved, front-line service employees must be made aware of the fact that they are important. SRC does it and so do most of the other exceptional service providers. Disney "works hard at making sure their employees know it (employee's job) is an important job and one that is respected and appreciated" [2]. Unless this happens, employees will soon develop an, "I just work here, don't look at me" attitude.

Front-line employees must be continually reminded of the value of customer service and of their own worth. A sense of self-worth and pride are important in service. Employees of the top-of-the-line service providers know they are important. They know service is important to the health of the corporation and that they directly impact the customer's perceptions. Maintenance, the cafeteria, personnel, accounting, sales, and part-time employees all impact customer perceptions and in turn, profits. This is an attitude that must be interwoven into the fabric of training our front-line service providers.

KEY POINTS

Training by itself is never enough to ensure quality service, but when it is done right it certainly is an important factor. Service training should be designed to help and encourage personnel to think on their feet. It should also be aimed at developing an appreciation for service and the important part each employee plays in delivering it. Career benefits and personal satisfaction should be tied directly to providing quality service. Self-image and self-worth and quality service are interrelated. They can be promoted through "ground up" promotion. They can be encouraged through monetary and nonmonetary incentives. They also can be promoted, as some do, through job rotation, front-line autonomy, and responsibility. Enhanced employee self-image and improved service can come about simply by explaining how the corporation's success rests on employees providing quality service. Whatever the means, it is essential that this message be effectively delivered.

Some key considerations when setting up an effective service training process include:

- Management needs to be committed to training
- Choose the right people as front-line service providers
- Believe in your personnel and treat them as if they were intelligent and competent (teach them about business and service)

- Act as a support group for employees by treating them fairly and as equals
- Stress the value of each person's job to quality service
- Promote self-confidence, self-respect, and a good self-image
- Teach, monitor, and review service courtesies
- Develop skills and attitudes needed to provide quality service (e.g., decision making, listening, adaptive behavior, stress management)

REFERENCES

1. Uttal, Bro., "Companies That Serve You Best," *Fortune*, Dec. 7, 1987, pp. 98–116.
2. Zemke, Ron, "Contact! Training Employees to Meet the Public," *Training*, Aug. 1986, pp. 41–45.
3. Lee, Chris, "Training the Front Line to Train the Front Line," *Training*, March 1987, pp. 77–81.
4. Robinson, Larry J. B., "Role Playing as a Sales Training Tool," *Harvard Business Review*, May–June 1987, pp. 34–35.

10

Incentives and Rewards

Quality service means intelligent use of incentives as well as intelligent training. When you train employees it is important to show them the connection between action and results. They have to have incentives. At SRC these consist of "Pac Man" type incentives, with each successively better performance "eating up" 10, 20, or 30% more money. They recognize that without incentives, you cannot appeal to an employee's natural desire for growth, need for challenges, and sense of ownership about their job and the company. In the long run you just cannot fool people. If it does not pay to work harder employees will respond with only minimum effort. Intelligence training means being honest. If it does not matter how hard one works because everybody is paid the same amount, then intelligent people will ask, "so why work harder?"

Few companies can match the sheer variety of incentives offered by American Express, a top service provider. They have over 100 programs for recognizing and rewarding personnel who take unusually good care of their customers. One program is the Great Performers award. It was instituted in 1982 and is designed to recognize those who go above and beyond the call of duty to help customers. Entry level employees up through directors at the corporate level are available for this recognition. However, it is more than volume that determines the success of incentives. It is the way they are organized. If incentives are to be effective they must be systematic rather than piecemeal. Everything must fit together.

One of the more intriguing and systematic uses of incentives to promote better productivity and service was introduced at American Airlines. The systematic use of incentives was part of an unusually successful employee suggestion program. Where most corporate employee suggestion programs fail, this one succeeded in a big way. In only three months of operation it saved the company over $50 million. Unlike many piecemeal approaches this program was well-organized. Every critical point along the way was tied into positive incentives. Rewards, feedback and logical organization were a vital part of their success.

In the twelve weeks from March 17, 1986 until June 20, 1986, American Airlines implemented an employee suggestion program they referred to as "InnovAAtions." It cost them between three to four million dollars to implement this extensive employee suggestion program but according to Bill Wallace, former administrator of the program, it was well worth the investment. Mr. Wallace said that they had expected to save between $18 and $20 million, but the program far exceeded expectations. He estimated that in the short time the program has been in operation it saved approximately $50 million.

This twelve-week program was so successful that in 1987 American Airlines introduced a long-term, permanent, company-wide employee suggestion program modeled after InnovAAtions. This new program, called "Ideas in Action," is based on the same procedures with a few minor changes. Since this new program has been in operation it has saved American Airlines an additional $6 million in 1987.

Undoubtedly, the employee suggestion program has been an unqualified success. It has succeeded when many company suggestion programs have traditionally been unsuccessful. For many companies, the "suggestion box" is a corporate joke. While many suggestion programs die for lack of interest, this one became extremely successful. What caused this success?

At the top of the list of reasons why this systematic program has worked while others have failed is top management commitment. Top management has consistently shown support for the program by providing the resources, consultants, and money to help develop the procedures for an effective suggestion program. They sponsored training for personnel in which videotapes emphasizing the need for and reasons for the suggestion program were shown. Management allowed "suggestion teams" to meet and discuss their ideas for improvement on company time. Most importantly though, top management demonstrated their commitment by making sure adequate resources and time were given to the program. As will be seen, this was no half-hearted effort.

Everyone at American Airlines knew that top management clearly supported the program. The program was first introduced to employees by their president and chairman, Robert L. Crandall. In videotapes he stressed the need to meet competitive challenges by "finding new ways to control expenses and generate revenue." He said the best way to find innovative approaches to doing this was to ask employees how to improve operations. His premise was that employees know their job better than anyone else. He told them that management would "listen, evaluate each idea, and respond in writing." He also made the point that if an employee's idea was used they would be eligible for a wide variety of incentives and rewards. He stressed that each employee could volunteer to be part of a team and each would be coached on techniques of building ideas. Most importantly Mr. Crandall pointed out that, "We'll listen, we'll respond—and provide awards."

As seen in Figure 10-1, almost 70% of those surveyed believed that management did support and encourage their participation. The message was clear: top management supports and encourages this program. Based on this foundation they developed a system to ensure the program's success.

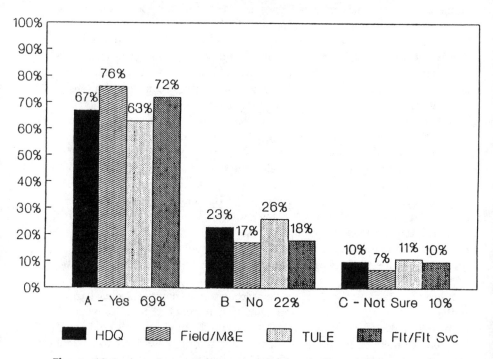

Figure 10-1. American Airlines employees believe management supports the employee suggestion program.

EXTENSIVE REWARDS

One of the more unusual and powerful cornerstones of their suggestion program was the extensive and systematic use of incentives as a means of generating ideas and suggestions. Both the process for encouraging ideas and the value of those rewards was significant. The result was that by the time the program had ended, 1,750 teams had been formed and generated 8,500 ideas, and 1,660 of these were approved. It was worth $4.7 million in prizes for participants. A key was that unlike many "stingy" suggestion programs, this one was designed to make it worthwhile to participate.

Participants even received rewards just for signing up to get involved. Prizes offered were based on money saved or revenue generated by the idea within one year. For instance, if an idea saved $500 to $1,499 in a year it was worth 3,750 Award Credits to each team member. Higher credits were given when larger amounts were saved. One flight attendant's team suggested substituting a two-cent pat of butter for a four-cent pat of jelly with croissants on all flights. The result was a savings of $20,000 for that year.

These credits are refundable for more than a thousand items in a merchandise book. To give you an idea of what award credits mean, consider these items from the catalog. If you want a "Weed Eater" it will cost 30,000 credits. A gas grill costs 59,000 credits. Titleist golf bags cost 14,000. A Samsung VCR costs 73,000 credits. The company also paid taxes associated with earning awards at a rate of 20%. Obviously these awards could "purchase" significant prizes.

Imagine what the flight attendant's team who suggested the $20,000 savings could do with the 93,750 credits it was worth to each participant. Even when the savings are shared among others within one's team, it is still a healthy incentive. No wonder there was significant participation!

It is not only the size of the incentives but also the distribution of rewards that has contributed to the program's success. Both the person originating the idea and almost everyone else connected with assessing and implementing it are rewarded for their efforts.

If an idea is accepted then every member of the team the person is on, as well as others connected with it, receive award credits. Team leaders who coordinate and schedule weekly team activities receive awards. Team coordinators who supervise an average of ten teams earn award credits for performing their job responsibilities as well as bonus award points when goals are met. The purpose was to encourage agreement and assistance to employees in preparing and submitting ideas as well as inspiring them to advocate ideas. Under the new program the supervisor of individuals who submit ideas also receives recognition award credits.

It is important to note this reward process also includes rewarding the Evaluation Committee that must approve or disapprove the idea. They are given credits for turnaround time for those ideas assigned to them. For instance, if their turnaround time is less than 14 days, the evaluation team would receive 60,000 credits; in taking 15 to 21 days they would get 37,000 credits; if it takes more than 29 days then they receive no credits.

Managers who must implement the idea also receive rewards for their efforts. Managers who put the ideas into effect share or split award credits with employees who are responsible for making the suggestion. Thus those who must change, who must implement the idea, are given award credits incentives when it is implemented. They have a direct stake in its success. As seen in Figure 10-2, this systematic approach did help generate ideas: 97% of American Airlines employees submitted ideas.

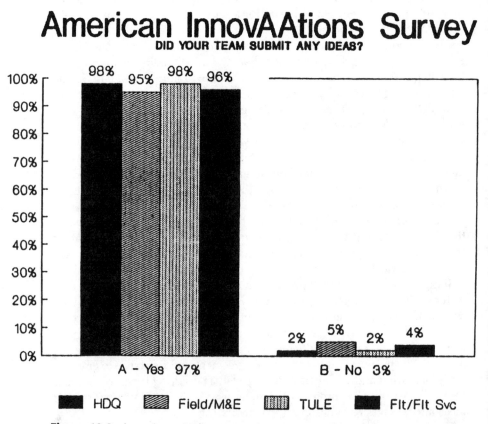

Figure 10-2. American Airlines employees contribute ideas to the program.

Feedback

Certainly one of the key reasons for the positive response of employees was the shared rewards, but probably of equal importance was the focus on feedback. As noted, the goal of the evaluation process was to try to reach a decision and notify the "suggester" in 14 days. If this deadline cannot be met, the evaluator must notify the suggester and provide status reports on the idea and expected completion dates. Team coordinators and others involved were also sent progress reports.

Although they rejected 70 % of the ideas, the emphasis was placed on being specific, respectful, and positive about the rejection. Typical eligible and ineligible ideas can be seen in Figures 10-3 and 10-4.

Preparation

Although the initial program only lasted twelve weeks, the preparation started months before the project was introduced to the company personnel. Extensive training, materials, and procedures were prepared. Program administrators and support personnel were documented and volunteers were assembled. When the program was introduced the evaluation committees that would assess the validity of the ideas had already been trained on how to evaluate ideas.

The first step was to form teams that would submit and document the ideas. Each team consisted of approximately seven members. They could be composed of those who worked together or not; however, the company preferred to have teams who shared a work interest.

Once an individual had submitted an idea then it became part of a system designed to ensure effective consideration and response. As seen in Figure 10-5, the idea would be documented and sent to a team coordinator who was responsible for overseeing several teams. As the idea was being logged in, the team coordinator sent a "We Have Your Idea" form (Figure 10-6) to the team leader and team. This feedback informed employees that their idea was actively being considered. Next the evaluation committee received and reviewed the idea. Sometimes this process meant that they would need additional information. In other cases it was either approved or disapproved.

If the idea was not approved the Evaluation Committee stated specific reasons why. If approved, the idea was assigned to an Implementation Manager and given a target implementation date. If the idea was approved it was also monitored by a Program Manager. Award credits (incentives) were then issued to both the Implementing Manager as well as the team generating the idea.

American Airlines' InnovAAtion program was successful because of its systematic use of incentives. It was not an amateurish approach. There was

---

IDEA CATEGORIES

Now that you understand how an idea flows within your location, you will want to make sure you understand the types of ideas that will impact American Airlines.

Eligible Ideas

Ideas which directly produce improvement in Company operations by reducing costs, generating profits or improving quality or safety are eligible for awards. Ideas dealing with the following areas of the business are generally considered eligible:

o Eliminate duplication of effort or paperwork and bottlenecks.

o Increase the profitability of existing products.

o Improve tools and equipment.

o Use materials now being scrapped.

o Simplify or improve procedures.

o Rearrange operations for better sequence and greater efficiency.

o Combine and eliminate operations.

o Simplify, eliminate or combine reports, records and letters.

o Reduce the frequency of equipment repairs.

o Substitute a less costly material without sacrificing quality.

o Make repairs or alterations at less cost.

o Identify new products/services.

o Identify other sources of revenue for American Airlines or other AA subsidiaries.

o Reduce the time needed to accomplish a task or job.

o Eliminate waste.

Figure 10-3. Samples of service improvement ideas considered eligible in the InnovAAtions program.

IDEA CATEGORIES (Cont.'d)

Ineligible Ideas

Generally speaking, ineligible ideas will fall into the following categories:

o Flight schedule changes.

o Route additions or deletions.

o Airline fares.

o Reduction of product quality or service levels.

o Conventional financings in public or private markets.

o Bank relations.

o Ideas not in keeping with the mission or image of American Airlines.

o Company personnel policy matters including matters covered by collective bargaining procedures.

o Employee benefit plans.

o Items related to advertising of our products or services or to the Company name and logo.

o Matters which could be corrected by complying with existing procedures.

o Suggestions that will produce a purely personal benefit.

o Matters related to "employees activities", such as recreational programs, physical fitness programs, and arts and crafts classes.

o Matters relating to termination of specific individuals.

o Matters already under consideration, due to either previously accepted suggestions or regular management function. Please refer to published list.

o Ideas which are not implementable within 12 months of submission.

o Regulatory, safety and legal matters governed by outside authority or circumstances.

o Ideas with first year net savings/net revenue of less than $500

Figure 10-4. Sample ideas not eligible in the InnovAAtions program.

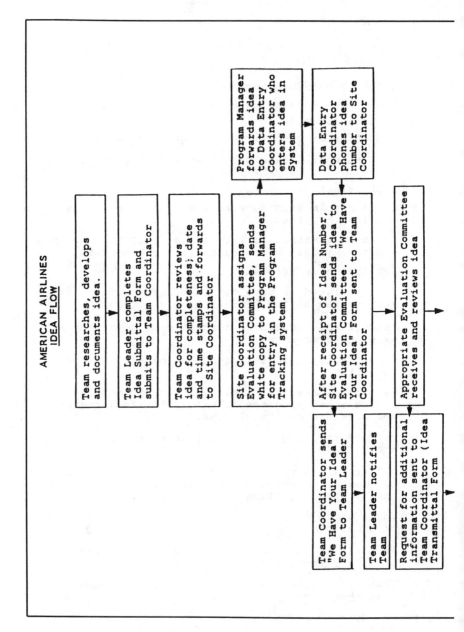

AMERICAN AIRLINES
IDEA FLOW

Team researches, develops and documents idea.

Team Leader completes Idea Submittal Form and submits to Team Coordinator

Team Coordinator reviews idea for completeness; date and time stamps and forwards to Site Coordinator

Site Coordinator assigns Evaluation Committee, sends white copy to Program Manager for entry in the Program Tracking system.

Program Manager forwards idea to Data Entry Coordinator who enters idea in System

Data Entry Coordinator phones idea number to Site Coordinator

After receipt of Idea Number, Site Coordinator sends idea to Evaluation Committee. "We Have Your Idea" Form sent to Team Coordinator

Team Coordinator sends "We Have Your Idea" Form to Team Leader

Team Leader notifies Team

Appropriate Evaluation Committee receives and reviews idea

Request for additional information sent to Team Coordinator (Idea Transmittal Form

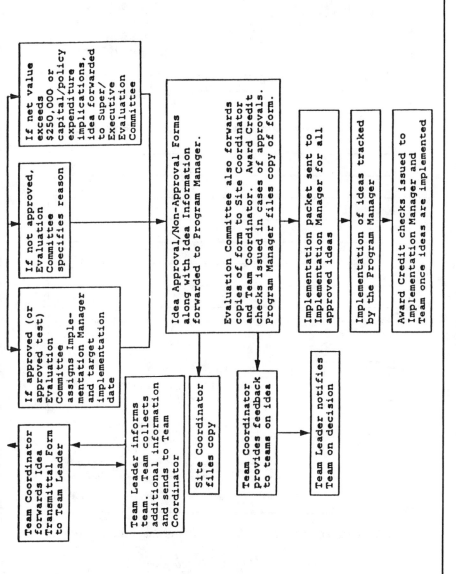

Figure 10-5. The service improvement idea under consideration.

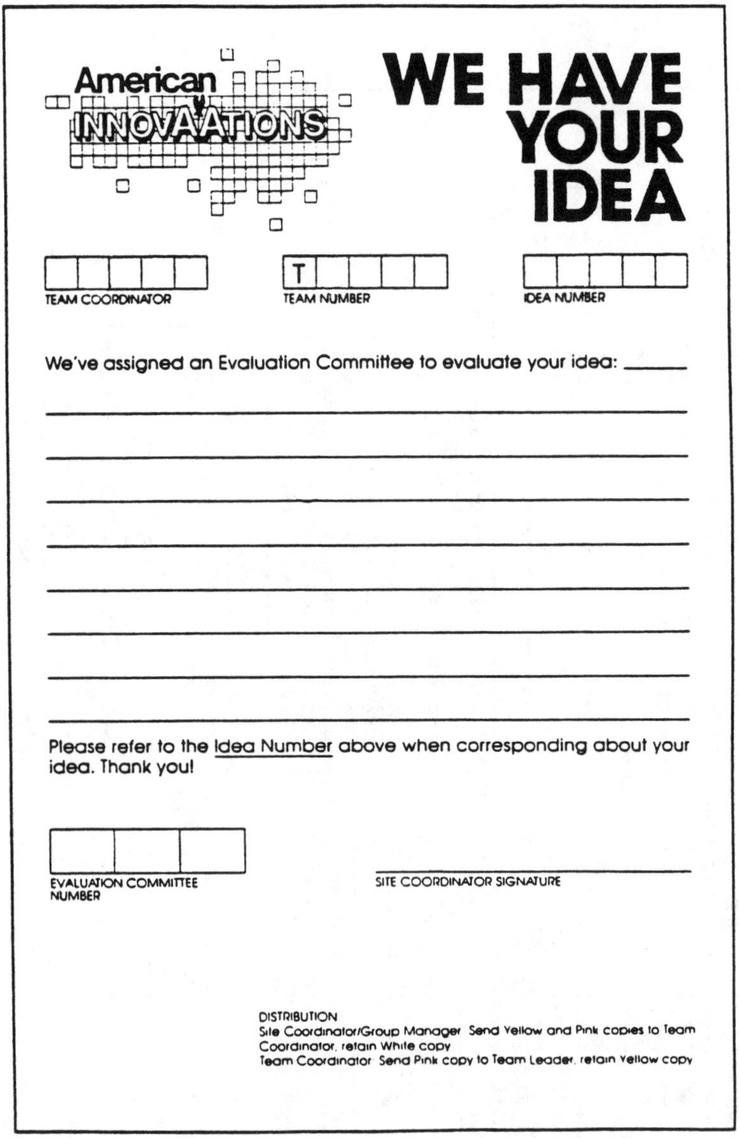

American INNOVAATIONS   **WE HAVE YOUR IDEA**

☐☐☐☐☐ TEAM COORDINATOR

T☐☐☐☐ TEAM NUMBER

☐☐☐☐☐ IDEA NUMBER

We've assigned an Evaluation Committee to evaluate your idea: _____

Please refer to the Idea Number above when corresponding about your idea. Thank you!

☐☐☐☐ EVALUATION COMMITTEE NUMBER

_____
SITE COORDINATOR SIGNATURE

DISTRIBUTION
Site Coordinator/Group Manager Send Yellow and Pink copies to Team Coordinator, retain White copy
Team Coordinator Send Pink copy to Team Leader, retain Yellow copy

Figure 10-6. Feedback forms are sent to teams that submitted ideas.

top management commitment. They developed a wide variety of incentives or a "reward menu" that appealed to the broadest possible group. The incentives were worth the effort and they were distributed fairly. Everyone had a direct stake in making the program work. They increased the probability of success by providing rapid reinforcement and turnaround on ideas that were suggested. In short, it took a great deal of front-end preparation, planning, and organization, but it was well worth the effort.

Although we will examine some common incentives used to enhance service, it is important to remember that the whole is more important than individual incentives. Regardless of the incentives used, it is more important that the whole program fit together to provide a clear focus. Whenever an incentive is introduced or eliminated, it should only be done within the context of the whole incentive package.

MONETARY INCENTIVES

One of the incentives that some excellent service providers use is pay. Many quality service providers like L.L. Bean, SRC, and Nordstrom, pay well. Nordstrom is the Seattle based department store that was mentioned in *Time* in 1987 as having exceedingly fast growth because they turned quality service into profits [1]. One of the major ingredients in their success is the fact that their salesclerks are paid 20% more than competitors' clerks. Not all, but many of the quality service providers seem to be of the opinion that if you pay for minimum wage help, that is just what kind of service you get—minimum.

Benefits

Employee benefits are another way of demonstrating management commitment to front-line employees. Benefits are sometimes used as a major tool to enhance service because they help develop a dedicated and loyal work force. Hallmark Cards Inc. has created a loyal and dedicated group of employees in part through their impressive benefit programs.

Hallmark has an excellent reputation for producing quality products. They are also ranked as one of America's best employers. Back in 1956 they created the Hallmark Career Reward Program. *Fortune* magazine called it, "the country's most liberal employee benefit and profit-sharing plan." Hallmark was selected as one of the country's top ten employers in the book, *The 100 Best Companies to Work for in America*, and in 1986 and 1987 *Working Mother* magazine chose it as one of "The 30 Best Companies to Work for in America." The reason for these praises in large part is due to Hallmark's benefits program.

Some of the benefits include: adoption assistance of up to $1,000; a referral service to help employees locate care for children, aging parents, or disabled family members; free refreshments during break; and low-interest $2,000-a-year college loans for children, with no payback until graduation. Hallmark also provides a physical fitness building at their corporate headquarters in Kansas City, Missouri.

The Nissan facility in Smyrna, Tennessee also has impressive benefits that revolve around a wellness program. Nissan's program is called Wellness in Nissan (WIN). They try to "facilitate individual's positive lifestyle change." A staff is available to present a workshop on WIN to any group that wants to hear about it. They offer on-going sessions every week for 30 minutes. WIN facilitators discuss integrating goal-setting principles into their daily work life. Spouses can become involved in the WIN program and participate in the work-group sessions.

Like Hallmark, Nissan also has an on-site fitness center. It includes everything from state-of-the-art Nautilus equipment to aerobic exercise, cross-country ski simulators, saunas, and other workout equipment. In addition to the wide array of physical fitness training, they also offer courses in karate, stress release techniques, and individual goal setting sessions. They also have a 57-acre recreational park that has an olympic-sized swimming pool.

Incentives are also at the heart of Wal-Mart's success. They have several types of incentives that allow their employees, whom they call "associates," a chance to become involved in the company's success and management. They, like L.L. Bean, SRC, and Hallmark, have several types of monetary and nonmonetary incentives for employees. Wal-Mart's incentives have one thing in common: like the American Airlines program, the goal is to get people involved so they feel they are a vital part of the organization.

One of the simpler but more effective incentives is the weekly monetary award given for effective merchandising. If a manager of one of their many store departments were to develop a merchandise presentation that resulted in good sales or profit for that area, she/he could submit the results to one of three divisions. The "winner" each week in each division receives a $50 check.

Another monetary incentive program is the Wal-Mart shrinkage program that offers a maximum of $200 to each full-time employee, and a prorated amount for each part-time employee depending on their time with the company. The $200 is given to these employees if the company achieves its shrinkage goals. Shrinkage has to do with the amount of inventory that "disappears" due to theft, improper counting, and so forth. For instance, if the company goal were one percent shrinkage of sales and the corporation were to come in at one percent then each store that qualified would receive the bonus. To qualify, a store has to improve or maintain the previous year's shrinkage.

Profit Sharing

Federal Express uses two types of profit sharing. One is normal profit sharing that goes into the employee's retirement program. The other is more unusual: merit profit sharing. To encourage performance, each year in June and December employees rate themselves in three different categories. For example, professional or exempt personnel are judged on

1. Professionalism, accuracy, and quality
2. Quality of work
3. Teamwork.

These employees can rate themselves from a minimum of one to a maximum of three in each of the categories. Their manager can also assign another point, so ten points is the maximum any employee can get.

Of course, managers consult with employees on this matter. In some cases rankings are lowered; in others, they are raised. These final rankings are then used to determine the amount of pay each employee will receive. This pay is thus based on individual ranking and the profits made by the corporation, and is in addition to normal pay and normal deferred profit sharing.

Companies like L.L. Bean, SRC, Hallmark, and Wal-Mart also recognize the benefits that profit sharing can have on employee motivation. All employees at Wal-Mart who work at least 1,000 hours a year are eligible for profit sharing in their second year of work. Money is deposited in an employee's account based on his/her gross earnings. More earnings means more money put into profit sharing. For example, assume corporate profit allowed an eight percent contribution to an employee's trust fund. This means that eight percent of the employee's gross eligible earnings would be added to his/her profit sharing trust fund. If an employee earned $10,000, then eight percent or $800 would be added to their trust account with no contribution by them. Those monies are then invested by trustees of that fund. This profit sharing system can produce significant income for employees when they retire. In turn, this provides long-term incentives and motivation for "associates" of Wal-Mart. It is not someone else's business; in part it belongs to the employee.

Like a strong benefits package, profit sharing is also important to Hallmark. Every year the corporation puts a certain percentage of their profits into an employee fund. It is usually invested in company stock. Employees own about one third of the business and the Hall family owns the rest. In 1987 the company put money equivalent to about 10.2% of an employee's salary into this profit sharing fund.

RECOGNITION, AWARDS, AND OTHER INCENTIVES

More difficult to quantify but just as important are nonmonetary incentives. As one store manager noted, "Everybody appreciates being appreciated." Wal-Mart management tries to make everyone feel that they are a vital part of the organization. Profit sharing helps but so does an occasional

"Thank you!" The company tries to make the stock people, cashiers, even those that bring in the shopping carts from the parking lot, feel like part of the organization. Wal-Mart tries to let them know if they have a "great idea." Even a smile helps.

As might be expected, Domino's Pizza uses local, regional, and national incentives to promote speed and product quality. They award plaques when a store's delivery time is consistently less than 25 minutes or below the national average. They have contests to make the "perfect pizza," and incentives for the best store of the month based on delivery times, product satisfaction, and image.

Plaques and cash awards are important for keeping up interest and participation but probably the most powerful incentives are the opportunities for *personal growth and challenge*. Since most of Domino's franchise organization members and store owners or managers were drivers or pizza makers, many employees recognize the potential for career advancement. Marty Prather, an A&M franchise owner, stated that his people know that if they do a good job they can own their own store in two or three years. A typical career path for them is seen in Figure 10-7. Now that is a real incentive!

Federal Express uses incentives to help them remain responsive. Like Domino's, they are aware of the need for personal growth and challenge. As already noted, 70% of their positions are filled internally. They also use other incentives to improve service performance. One of these is their "pay for performance" program. It is designed to reduce the problems associated with the traditional step-by-step pay process that is based on length of service. With Federal Express's incentive program, if an employee does get to the top of a work-experience pay scale, he or she is still eligible for merit performance pay based on service achievements.

Federal Express also uses individual service incentives such as the Bravo Zulu Voucher program. (The name is based on the Bravo Zulu flag used by the U.S. Navy to mean "well done.") Monetary and nonmonetary awards (sports and theater tickets, dinner for two) are awarded to employees who show "exemplary performance." There is very little red tape because individual managers use their own discretion.

More formal programs include the Golden Falcon Award. This award is given to those who demonstrate service to the customer that goes "above and beyond the call of duty." A committee nominates and selects candidates each month and the winner receives a lapel pin as a token of appreciation, as well as Federal Express common stock. These programs, along with Federal Express's "no layoff" policy, are powerful encouragements.

Hallmark, Wal-Mart, SRC, L.L. Bean, Pepsi-Cola General Bottlers, Inc., and Nordstrom are also able to motivate quality service by monetary and nonmonetary means. They congratulate and encourage front-line employees. References in all of these organizations are made to "family." They are

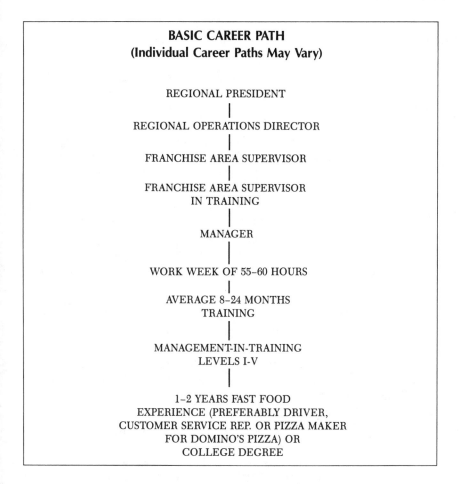

BASIC CAREER PATH
(Individual Career Paths May Vary)

REGIONAL PRESIDENT
|
REGIONAL OPERATIONS DIRECTOR
|
FRANCHISE AREA SUPERVISOR
|
FRANCHISE AREA SUPERVISOR
IN TRAINING
|
MANAGER
|
WORK WEEK OF 55–60 HOURS
|
AVERAGE 8–24 MONTHS
TRAINING
|
MANAGEMENT-IN-TRAINING
LEVELS I-V
|
1–2 YEARS FAST FOOD
EXPERIENCE (PREFERABLY DRIVER,
CUSTOMER SERVICE REP. OR PIZZA MAKER
FOR DOMINO'S PIZZA) OR
COLLEGE DEGREE

Figure 10-7. Sample career path of a Domino's Pizza employee.

more than employees and management; they are a unit, and no price can be put on that.

Those intangibles are hard to define, but what is clear is that effective service management makes a point of staying in contact with employees. Managers need to make a policy of working beside their employees, listening to their ideas, and giving them accountability and responsibility. Wal-Mart store manager Ralph Graham noted than 73% of all the merchandise sold was purchased by employees and various department managers. Employees were responsible for replenishment of the store inventory. That kind of decentralized autonomy is unusual in most establishments, but it is a powerful incentive for quality service. It is also one of the secrets of many of our organizations' successes.

KEY POINTS

Incentives for providing quality service are essential. As with training, incentives help move decision making further down through the organization and in turn produce a more responsive and effective organization. Service is people, and incentives should be focused on promoting their efforts.

There are many types and combinations of service-encouraging incentives available, including monetary and nonmonetary ones. The key to their effectiveness is not their existence or type but rather the way they are used. The three most important words that best describe effective use of incentives are commitment, commitment, and commitment. Top management must demonstrate support and commitment. There are a variety of ways to do this. One way is money. As the old adage goes, "You get what you pay for." As already seen, many of the top service providers obtain employee effort and commitment because the company has earned it through their wages and/or benefit programs.

Profit sharing is one of the more popular and effective incentives (e.g., L.L. Bean, SRC, Hallmark). It gives everyone a direct stake in the profits and success of the company. It is not just someone else's business, it is theirs. However, this alone is not enough. In fact, it does not have to exist in order for a company to supply effective service (e.g., McDonald's). Successful use of incentives also involves nonmonetary ones. Some of the nonmonetary techniques mentioned here include giving front-line service providers additional responsibility, accountability, and participation in decision making. Smiles, encouragement, and so forth are valuable, but again, these practices are not enough.

What is required for incentives to be effective is support and planning. Management must show commitment to them as in American Airlines' case and in other cases like Hallmark's where obvious liberal benefits provide proof of the company's commitment. Beyond this support is a need for preparation. Incentives are a powerful means of changing behavior, but change will only occur if they are not administered haphazardly. Many a merit pay plan has failed because not enough planning and organizing occurred early on. A little extra time here saves a lot of effort later.

The objectives should be to make the incentives as systematic as possible. Develop a wide variety of incentives that appeal to as many as possible. Develop individual incentives like profit sharing that have strong appeal to almost everyone. Make incentives worth the effort. The effort, as in American Airlines' case, will be paid back many times over. Give employees a chance to control their own effort and exercise individual initiative and creativity at delivering services. Provide frequent and rapid feedback on efforts and performance. Reward all personnel for quality service. This includes those directly and indirectly involved. When all of the pieces are focused in the same direction, a powerful tool is available for enhancing quality service.

Some specific suggestions for effective incentives include:

- Top management must demonstrate support
- Spend necessary time preparing and organizing the who, what, where, when and whys of incentives
- Make incentives systematic and logical
- All involved directly and indirectly with incentives should receive incentives
- Give incentives that connect action to results
- Use incentives that appeal to a wide variety of personnel
- Make their efforts worthwhile
- Provide frequent and rapid feedback on performance

REFERENCE

1. Russell, George, "Where the Customer is Still King," *Time*, February 2, 1987, p. 56.

11

Decentralization

Every organization approaches customer service from its own unique perspective. However, one thing is common to all services: the need for decentralization. Frequently customer complaints and dissatisfied customers occur because the service person dealing with the customer lacks the authority to help the customer.

The idea is to create small areas within the organization that can be given profit and loss responsibility. If services can be divided into small incentive sections, it is easier to instill the service mentality essential for quality service and customer satisfaction.

There are many examples of quality service providers improving their service mentality through various forms of decentralized management. We have already looked at SRC, Wal-Mart, and other organizations' decentralized approaches, including Federal Express's use of only five levels of management. There are many others. For instance, Nordstrom, the Seattle department store, uses their own form of decentralized management to improve service mentality.

Nordstrom's decentralized system is set up so department, store, and regional managers are free to make their own decisions. In fact, each region has its own buyers to ensure that each is responsive to particular regional tastes and needs. Even the design of stores is decentralized. Each Nordstrom store is designed to complement its geographical and economic environment. Approximately 70% of their merchandise is available in all stores, but the rest is unique to each store or region. This is a considerable variation, considering they are primarily a West Coast entity.

Their decentralized philosophy extends to the sales floor. Each of the salespeople develops his/her own client list and operates on a base wage plus a commission on all sales they make. Salespeople handle complaints and merchandise returns as well as sales. Instead of returning merchandise to one centralized area, at Nordstrom, customers return an item where they purchased it. Such a decentralized approach is in stark contrast to many poor service retail stores.

PROJECTS, CIRCLES, AND TEAMS

Projects, circles, teams and other such "add on" arrangements are ways many organizations try, with varying degrees of success, to incorporate a decentralized perspective within their organization. Weyerhaeuser is a forest products, paper, and real estate company that went through a major turnaround in their business outlook, in part due to a change in managerial style. In the boom years of the late 1970s, with rapidly inflating timber values, the company was a highly integrated operation designed to squeeze the highest value from each tree [1]. This required a lot of complex planning and reporting which resulted in a large corporate and business staff. When the market changed Weyerhaeuser had to also make some changes to remain prosperous.

Today George H. Weyerhaeuser, CEO of the company, noted, "Our business is organized into three major stand-alone groupings which operate essentially as if they were separate companies, with entrepreneurial operating units" [1]. As a result, the number of staff and supervisory personnel "shrank sharply and flattened out." He noted that because of their quality improvement efforts, hourly workers, working in teams, are able to do much of the planning and control formerly imposed on them, and they are doing it better. Quality and productivity are up, costs are down, and morale is high.

Another organization that uses a form of decentralized management to enhance quality is Nissan. They have 55 involvement circles in their plant in Smyrna, Tennessee. The circles allow employees opportunities to participate in problem solving and decision making. They are voluntary and average about 10 members each and meet an hour a week during work hours on paid overtime. All circle leaders and facilitators receive 20 hours of training in problem solving, listening skills, conducting effective meetings, and team building. These circles have received management approval to implement solutions to over 90 problems involving quality, safety, and productivity concerns.

AT&T is yet another service provider that has seen the positive effect of a decentralized approach. Their AT&T Components and Electronic Systems Reading Works produces a variety of electronic devices. For several years the plant suffered from labor unrest. Their technical and professional employees were so dissatisfied that productivity suffered. Many felt that the corporate organization was not letting them have a say in decisions affecting their jobs.

Today, teams of personnel at all levels make decisions on how to operate the business. Over 45 project teams have been formed to investigate a wide variety of issues including appraisal process, building security, pension plans, and computer resources available to personnel. The result has been increased productivity and quality, as well as improvement on the financial side [1].

Add-on approaches to decentralized management where teams, circles, and projects are created have met with varying success. To be truly successful with decentralized management one must change the entire structure of the organization. Responsive and effective service demands a decentralized philosophy throughout the organization. We have already documented Domino's approach, but other service providers use what might be referred to as responsible autonomy.

RESPONSIBLE AUTONOMY

The success of many of the top service providers can partly be attributed to a philosophy of *responsible autonomy*. It is a decentralized managerial approach that allows individual managers the flexibility to manage their operations while still maintaining corporate accountability. It provides managers with a feeling of ownership while leaving ultimate control in the hands of the corporation.

Many companies today are experimenting with this concept of responsible autonomy as a way of improving service. Zale Corporation (jewelry stores) has increased the autonomy of their three major divisions so they are 100% responsible for what goes on in those divisions [2].

Polaroid's Consumer Resource Center, which is their facility designed to handle customer complaints, uses a form of responsible autonomy. They adopted very flexible guidelines where representatives have latitude to do whatever is necessary to make their customers happy. Digital Equipment Corporation uses a manager of quality who responds directly to a corporate executive committee. The manager has a mandate to do whatever is necessary to improve service, product quality, and customer satisfaction [3].

Perhaps one of the more interesting examples of how responsible autonomy can improve service was demonstrated by Byerly's, the up-scale Minneapolis based grocery stores, written up in *Time* magazine. Their success as a top-notch quality service provider is in large part due to their decentralized management that focuses on responsible autonomy. The article noted that while Byerly's stores are attractive looking, the difference is in the way they are managed. "Each store is managed semi-independently by a single boss" [4]. The general manager at each Byerly's store sets prices and designs the product assortment. Don Byerly, president of the company, noted that, "We have an extremely decentralized management structure." For instance, he emphasized that the person running the produce department does his own buying, pricing, and hiring. He said it really is their "own business and that they have been lucky enough to find entrepreneurial types" [5].

Supermarket News reported that the management believes that by operating their stores autonomously and not dictating buying policies from headquarters they have "flexibility to move very quickly on customer requests" [5]. Like Nordstrom, Byerly's also has stores in areas that have specific needs. Because there are differences in customer mix and different product requirements, store management has the authority to make buying decisions based on those needs. They believe their decentralized approach has made it easier to change with the trends. Decentralization has allowed them to respond very quickly to changing customer wants and needs.

One other example of a service organization that epitomizes this decentralized approach is Harte-Hanks Communication. They own and operate a wide range of communication organizations throughout the United States. They own television stations, newspapers, radio stations, advertising publications, cable television systems, and other entertainment programming. Three of the four television stations they own are number one in their markets and the fourth is number two.

In following the philosophy of responsible autonomy, as long as respective stations remain successful, they have a great deal of flexibility in running their operations. If problems do occur, the corporation headquarters will expect improvement. They suggest possible answers, but individual managers still have flexibility in developing solutions. The corporation believes that local managers know their market better than anyone else. One manager said he and others feel a sense of commitment when the corporation says, "It's yours; do the best you can." He went on to say, "There isn't someone constantly looking over your shoulder. No one is running around fearful about their job."

This corporation's form of decentralized management, like the previous examples, resembles a cross between self-employed ownership and corporate control. It works primarily because of the managers chosen to run the operations. They sincerely try to find managers who have the right stuff. A great deal of attention is given to not only finding the best top manager to run the station, but also to finding the best managers at all levels. One station manager notes that they want managers with personalities that fit in with others within the organization. They want people who have an aptitude for creativity, who are problem solvers and who are intelligent.

Most importantly, they want to know how prospective managers feel about themselves and others. They want people who feel good about themselves and who feel good about other people. To help insure this, one station manager uses a consulting psychologist to evaluate prospective managers. He went on to say he could only recall one case where a recommended manager did not work out. He remarked that no system is perfect, but for him using a psychologist has been successful.

Responsible autonomy works best when there is a match between corporate and personal style. One successful manager in the Harte-Hanks Communications system is an example of this match. He exemplifies the decentralized manager, stating "I am not smart enough to do it all." He obviously is smart enough but chooses to distribute power to subordinate managers.

Shortly after he became general manager he formed a management team. It consisted of the eight key managers at the station. Jointly these managers set all policies for the company. Each of these managers sets their own department goal in consultation with the general manager. Each manager exercises considerable autonomy within their area. For example, the program manager, not the general manager, determines what movies the station will schedule. Likewise, the sales manager, not the general manager, sets the rates for advertising.

SRC, a corporation previously mentioned, has its own form of budgetary decentralized management. We noted that SRC training programs focus on pushing decision-making authority down through the organization. As noted in Chapter 9, difficult tasks were formerly administered by middle and upper management. Today the majority of those difficult tasks are performed by floor managers.

You might assume that a decentralized approach, where employees and front-line managers take greater responsibility for planning, organizing, and controlling their work areas, would require considerably more time for decision-implementation than a highly centralized approach. Not so, according to Gary Brown, Human Resources Director at SRC. "All we (upper management) have to do is to look at the bottom number; we just compare what they are doing to our financial and income statements."

The ability to simply rely on the judgment of front-line people requires a great deal of trust. This trust is built on the knowledge that each person responsible and accountable for management expenses has been shown how they relate to the company's bottom line and how to manage those resources.

Brown demonstrates this trust when he notes that they do not triple-check figures. "We take the person's word for it. He (the employee) has all the numbers." The attitude that runs up as well as down the organization is "if you knew what I knew, you would make the same decision I did." With this type of trust, it is easy to see how speed can be increased.

Of course, this approach did not come about overnight, and it is not strictly limited to budgetary aspects. At one time Jack Stack, President and CEO at SRC, approved all overtime. If a supervisor wanted to work on Saturday, he or she had to submit a list of those who were going to work overtime and then list the reasons why the overtime was needed. As the company grew, it became impossible for Stack to continue to do this. At first this responsibility was given to Mike Carrigan, the vice president, but slowly, over the years, it moved down through the organization.

Today the front-line manager decides when to work overtime based on the production schedule. Usually the production manager only advises the front-line supervisor if he knows about something that might affect the decision. For instance, a supervisor may have scheduled overtime on a product but the production manager lets them know that the product will not be shipped for another three weeks; thus it is not necessary to work overtime.

At one time scheduling of work was performed at the highest management level. Today that responsibility has been delegated downward to the production scheduler and parts expeditor (non-exempt, basically clerical employee). Upper management taught those employees the business parameters of scheduling delivery of parts (the faster it goes, the more it costs), and then gave them the responsibility and authority to do the job.

Wal-Mart, like SRC, Byerly's, Nordstrom and other top service providers, encourages individual responsibility for their department personnel. One store manager said the snack bar department manager, like other managers at the store, places his own orders for supplies. Store managers send orders in to the vendor, but no one approves them who knows better about what is needed. Department managers decide what merchandise will be ordered and how much.

Store managers encourage this responsibility and accountability through open communication. Each department manager knows his sales and payroll, among other key indexes, as well as where his department ranks among similar departments within the region. These managers are responsible for purchasing the majority of store merchandise. Compare this decentralized approach to those of most discount merchandisers where the corporate office does the exclusive buying.

DECENTRALIZATION THROUGH QWL

Each of these companies has had great success with their forms of responsible autonomy, but one of the most intriguing examples of decentralized management on a large scale was introduced by American Airlines. This organization has a reputation for service and on-time delivery. A few years ago they began experimenting with their own brand of decentralized management. At American Airlines this goes under the title of Quality of Work Life (QWL).

Many companies are experimenting today with QWL programs, which are designed to enhance the work life of employees. The aim is usually to get greater participation and involvement from employees in the decision-making process. While many companies may recognize the benefits of greater employee involvement, many also treat it as a project rather than a process. Some jump on the bandwagon as they would any fad. Some do it in a piecemeal approach. Some even develop detailed procedures but get little action. Others send out corporate memos but do not take their message seriously.

American Airlines began implementing this decentralized management process in 1983 and today continues to expand its scope. It is a serious attempt to change the way the corporation is run. They hope to obtain employee involvement and participation in the decision-making that affects those employees' jobs. They want to create a corporate culture that tries to make every person an "active partner." A decision was made by management to share the responsibility of running the company with the employees.

The process has produced some positive results. As mentioned, they recently introduced a three-month employee suggestion program requesting ideas for improvement. The result was that 97% of their "suggestion teams" submitted ideas that saved the company over $50 million. Another suggestion program has saved an additional $6 million in seven months.

In Salt Lake City, a group suggested creating a special airport service using college students (called ski patrol) to help improve check-in procedures. Another group suggested a floating holiday that involved volunteering to work a holiday in exchange for a day off of the agent's choice. The result was an estimated $43,000 savings for one holiday alone. In another qualitivity case, American Airlines mechanics literally hand-built some of their handling equipment, which costs less to maintain and operates more efficiently than the original equipment.

In Lubbock, employees have been voluntarily working some days off in another job function so they can better understand service problems. In Tulsa, the Fleet Operating Engineering employees participated in the layout, design, and equipping of new areas. Fleet service clerks in Philadelphia developed a better baggage-sorting system. Amarillo employees choose fellow workers for "employee of the quarter" honors. Some employees are even designing their own performance appraisal forms.

Changing the Way People Behave

Obviously this company has had success with their decentralized process and they expect more of it in the future. President and Chairman of American Airlines, R. L. Crandall, believes it is the "way of the future." He has been quoted as saying, "Participative management is not a passing fancy . . . employee morale makes all the difference and we can never return to doing things the old way."

It is not easy to change a corporate culture, but that is what it takes to successfully change the way people behave toward each other. Marsha Raulston, co-coordinator of QWL, notes that they have been successful at making changes because they "see it as a cultural change within the organization." She believes this process is more basic than rules, regulations, policies, and procedures. The biggest thing is to "change the way we behave toward each other and the way we interact with each other on a day-to-day basis." Changing the culture begins at the top. If change is to prosper, it must have top management support. Top management sets the tone for everything. Chairman Crandall describes QWL as "trust, cooperation, communication, and mutual support." Crandall makes it clear to personnel that "QWL will continue to receive the full support of their top management." Marsha Raulston emphasized that if you ask anyone in this company if the president believes in this process not one person would say he was not behind it.

EMPLOYEE INVOLVEMENT

One reason for American Airlines' success with their own form of decentralized management is their extensive training process for both management and employees. Like Nissan and others, their focus is on training managers to function in a more participatory environment. They believe the way people react to others is built on old habits and it takes training to change those habits.

Coordinators of this process noted that if employees are not properly trained, then no amount of managerial support will help. They emphasize problem solving skills in training. They believe, for instance, that it is unwise to ask an aircraft cleaner to participate if he or she has never been trained in how to solve problems. An employee cannot participate in decision making if he/she does not know how.

Another type of training has also been valuable. It assumes a different management style is necessary if the goal is to bring employees into the decision-making process. They believe a partnership requires a more democratic leadership style. As one noted, "One can't share decision-making responsibility and still remain autocratic."

This type of leadership training or approach is called "Peak Performance Through Commitment." It aims to encourage good performance and improve the performance of those who need it. The focus is on reinforcing good behavior and correcting poor performance in a positive manner. To this end American Airlines has tried to dismantle their old disciplinary program. They even threw out their old disciplinary form. The message from corporate headquarters is, "Don't do that anymore—don't issue disciplinary forms."

Jay McCormick, co-coordinator of QWL, said the company has gone to a coaching and counseling approach to discipline as opposed to the traditional way. He said in the past when someone made a mistake the attitude was, "O.K. you've made a mistake, don't do it again." Now the approach is,

"Let's sit down and talk about why you made this mistake so we can understand what went wrong and how we can help." This type of approach is in contrast to giving a first warning, a second warning (and time off), and then firing an employee if a third warning occurs. McCormick emphasized that the new approach is to create an environment that says, "We do care—our goal is not to fire you, it is to correct the problem so you (employee) will stay a part of the company."

In these training sessions, managers are told there are some new behaviors they need to exhibit rather than handing employees several forms to fill out. In the training session it is emphasized that if a manager wants someone to do better, then he/she should coach and counsel. They believe the outcome of this process is committed employees. The emphasis is on having employees participate in the process.

COMMUNICATION

Another aspect of American Airlines' program is communication. Bill Shannon, senior vice-president of field sales and service, said, "Communication is essential to get things going." This company recognizes that it is essential to getting their message to their people if they want to change the culture. Therefore, they continue to publicize the process. They have sponsored seminars attended by mostly non-management employees who voluntarily participated on one of their days off. At this meeting they listened to speeches and had the opportunity to describe what they were doing to promote decentralized management. The company also promotes the process in its company newspaper. It highlights success stories and lets others know how employees throughout the company are participating in decision making.

The corporate staff also make themselves available and accessible to assist employees throughout the company. Any employee can call for assistance in implementing the program. The staff will respond if mechanics, flight attendants, or anyone else wants them to come to an area to explain the concept or assist if they are having difficulty. At the heart of this communication process is the recognition that communication involves more than talking. They are trying to build grass-roots support rather than issuing manuals, procedures, and directives. In 1986, American Airlines initiated an employee survey to gauge how employees felt about opportunities to communicate and participate. The company was trying to assess fairness and to see how they were doing. The results were positive, but the important message lay in showing that they were listening to their employees. The objective in future surveys will be to listen and improve.

Stan Pederson, the president and general manager of the Harte-Hanks television station, also recognized that the responsible autonomy approach to decentralization requires a great deal of communication and team play. He continually encourages his department managers to avoid turf building and to get their own personnel involved in the problem-solving process. The major way they do this is through communication. They enhance communication efforts by being open with their personnel. Every Wednesday they have a "manager's meeting." It is designed as an informational meeting to keep department managers informed about various aspects of the organization. Additionally, they also post the minutes of each of these meetings for all employees to see. In this manner employees are kept informed about what is going on within the organization.

Pederson also emphasizes open communication by encouraging regular department meetings where employees can voice concerns. In these meetings managers are encouraged not to review anything that employees already know. He believes that many employees do not like to go to meetings because managers frequently end up reviewing things that employees already know about and avoid subjects that might lead to controversy.

Each manager is further encouraged to seek employees' views. If employees ask for something, managers are supposed to be honest with them. "If necessary, tell them why it cannot be done." Pederson realizes everyone will not get everything they ask for but, above all, he does not want his managers to tell an employee, "It's not in the budget." He believes that if a manager makes this statement, or similar remarks, it prevents discussion of the proposal. In the short run it ends the discussion, but in the long run it "kills initiative and creativity."

To help isolate areas of improvement Harte-Hanks conducted a "climate survey" that identified a range of employee attitudes. This information, along with other results, was collected and department sessions were conducted to determine what specific incidents had created some degree of unhappiness. As a result of these meetings, the general manager instituted changes aimed at setting up programs for: individual recognition, identifying job performance, improving training, evaluating and restructuring the pay scale, improving the content of department meetings, and being more open about organizational decisions. Those are not just words, those are actions that demonstrate a commitment to decentralized management.

Mike Carrigan, vice president of SRC, may have said it best when he emphasized, "We set a corporate program of open communication; we share everything with our employees. If people feel they have a right and an obligation to communicate, it makes them grow. It makes them more precise about what they communicate (to each other and the customer)."

The chairman of American Airlines said the program of decentralized management started with the idea that many workplace problems can be solved most effectively from the bottom up rather than the top down. The point was that different operations have different needs and who better knows those needs than local personnel. Today they continue to try and convince other managerial personnel that the "experts on a function are the ones who do the job."

Like many top service providers, American Airlines believes that before procedures, policies, and changes are made you should consult the experts (employees). As a result of this philosophy, the company today has far more task forces, committees, and up-front employee decision making than ever before. For example, when they decided to look at new uniforms for ticket agents the first thing done was to ask those who must wear them every day to participate in an ongoing task force. As Raulston said, "We want these people involved in making decisions, not some purchasing agent sitting in a vacuum."

They have also helped form work groups so that participation can be improved. These work groups consist of people doing the same thing but in different locations. They are encouraged to form these groups so they can communicate with each other about similar concerns. Flight attendants, pilots, and some freight groups have done this so they know what each is doing and can improve their input to the decision-making process.

As noted earlier, some employees are also getting involved in developing their own performance evaluation. Task forces were formed when the company went around to some of the employees and asked them "What's important to you? What should we be looking at when we do these evaluations?" Jay McCormick mentioned that, basically, ticket agents designed their own performance evaluation. Currently other employees are looking at such areas as flex-benefits.

Employees are also setting up some recognition systems at the local level. If a local area wants to recognize a person for handling customers in some way, they can do it. Currently the company is also trying to put together a corporate-wide recognition system so that the corporation can recognize special efforts. For instance, if a pilot sees a mechanic do something and wants to recognize him—how does he do it? How can he say "nice job"? That is what the corporation is currently trying to do. The company is not worried that employees will be inconsistent about why they reward someone. McCormick notes, "They (employees) put together a more difficult (comprehensive) program than I would."

KEY POINTS

What is apparent from these experiences is that it takes several ingredients to be successful with decentralized service. Of utmost importance is top management support. However, it is deeds, not talk, that matter. SRC and American Airlines back up directives from upper management by encouraging extensive training to enhance employee ability to participate in decision making. They have spent the time training managers to coach rather than discipline and they continue to communicate their success and philosophy throughout the organization.

They have been successful because they showed that sharing responsibility and accountability was not a "one-shot" program. Instead they aim to create a cultural process that will reshape the way they manage. To that end they have developed new employee performance programs. American Airlines introduced two extremely successful employee suggestion programs called "InnovAAtions" and "Ideas in Action." Likewise, there are career development programs and, above all, there is emphasis on communication.

It involves talking to and listening to employees. It means encouraging them to form groups to communicate concerns to management and to make proposals on how to make things better. As McCormick and Raulston of American Airlines say, it involves listening to proposals and taking action and demonstrating support.

Some of the key considerations when improving services through decentralization include:

- Develop a service mentality in personnel by dividing service functions into small incentive-based sections that are both accountable and responsible for service.
- Encourage personnel to handle all job functions, including ordering, complaint handling and returns, as well as sales.
- Develop employee decision teams that are responsible for the planning and control of each task.
- Encourage responsible autonomy in all personnel by giving wide latitude, authority, and responsibility to solve problems.
- Find the right "entrepreneurial types" who feel good about themselves and others so it is easier to implement a decentralized approach to service.
- Coach, counsel, and encourage rather than discipline.
- Teach personnel how to participate by teaching them about the organization, about leadership skills, about solving problems and decision making, about listening and, in general, how to build team efforts.
- Make everyone an active partner in service by developing and encouraging open communication between levels and among personnel.
- Have top management demonstrate support for decentralization of service responsibility and accountability.

REFERENCES

1. "Quality: The Competitive Advantage," (Paid Advertising Section), *Fortune,* September 28, 1987.

2. Zale, Donald, "The Need to Rekindle the Entrepreneurial Spirit," *Zale Retailing Issues Letter*, Vol. II, No. 3, September, 1986.
3. U.S. Office of Consumer Affairs, "Increasing Customer Satisfaction: Through Effective Corporate Complaint Handling," (Washington: Government Printing Office).
4. Russell, George, "Where the Customer is Still King," *Time*, February 2, 1987, p. 56.
5. Davis, Tim, "Byerly's Building Upscale Opportunities," *Supermarket News*, Vol. 37, No. 28, July 13, 1987, p. 11.

12

Principles of Quality Service

Sometimes in America it seems there are two kinds of service: self-service and no service at all. Generally speaking, service is in a sorry state and consumers are fed up with it. More and more businesses are realizing the importance service plays in their future success. This book is about many of those on the cutting edge of service and how they are able to become and remain highly successful through quality service.

One thing to keep in mind though, as I said earlier, is that there are no "10s" when it comes to service. Undoubtedly customers will, as I have done, stand in line too long at a "top service provider."

There will be times some of those with reputations for service will lose baggage, or take too long to process paperwork, or greet customers in a rude, uncaring, or bureaucratic manner. Although there are surely exceptions, most of these service providers have exceedingly high service levels. Ninety-eight and ninety-nine-percent-plus seems to be the rule and 100% service is the goal.

These numbers did not occur by accident. It is not image; it is real. It was not developed by marketing, and money is not enough to buy it. It is basic good management. Earlier I said service stinks because often front-line service jobs stink. We can carry that one step further; often service stinks because of the lack of effective management.

Top service companies are able to effectively deliver service because they apply the basic principles of quality service. These principles—not promotions, not money, not corporate directives—are the heart and soul of quality service.

PRINCIPLE 1
MANAGERIAL VISION

What do Joyce C. Hall, Jack Stack, Sam Walton, Leon Leonwood Bean, and Thomas Monaghan have in common? They were or are CEOs of their respective organizations who were able to share their vision of how their business should be run. The ability to impart their unique vision for their organizations is what separates them from most top management. To develop a unique approach the CEO must first have a vision for the way things should be, then have the ability to get others within the organization to accept that vision. The CEO's vision and the ability to impart it to others is the glue that binds all the other pieces of the customer satisfaction puzzle together.

The lack of this vision and its effect can be readily seen in the case of Domino's pizza. The organization went through two crises, both of which almost destroyed the organization. One of those was in the mid-1960s and the other was in the early 1970s. The crises, in both cases, came down to strategy and a lack of managerial vision.

In the mid-1960s Monaghan had a partner who wanted to provide a regular restaurant atmosphere rather than the streamlined philosophy of Domino's. There were two separate visions for what the restaurant should be and there were two separate strategies for accomplishing it. This "split personality" referred to in Chapter 5 nearly destroyed Domino's. Things only got better when Monaghan and his partner split and Monaghan began developing his unique, simplified, and specialized approach.

Later in the 1970s managerial vision, or rather the lack of it, again created a crisis. Monaghan wanted to step aside and leave much of the day-to-day running of the organization to others. He brought in outside managers to run the organization. These people were professional managers with restaurant experience; however, they were unfamiliar with the unique philosophy of Domino's. These managers lost touch with the franchise owners and operators. The business sputtered and was in serious trouble. Lawsuits and debts were incurred. It was only when Monaghan resumed leadership of the corporation that Domino's path became clear and the business recovered.

Domino's story of corporate vision is not unique. Whenever there is a change in leadership it is always a time of crisis. In the case of most of our quality service providers, it has been successfully passed. L.L. Bean went through a crisis when their founder died in the mid-1960's and his grandson, Leon A. Gorman, assumed leadership. As seen in chapter four, this crisis was successfully overcome. In fact, Gorman is given most of the credit for revitalizing the organization. He kept what had worked in the past (service) and then went on to create a growing dynamic organization.

When Sam Walton handed over the day-to-day leadership to David Glass, there was some concern, but most felt Glass was cut in the same mold as Walton. Still, under Walton's vision and guiding hand, Wal-Mart remains a force within the discount store business.

When Hall of Hallmark fame died there was also a crisis, but since approximately two-thirds of the business and the leadership were still in family hands, their business retained its unique personality. These stories of managerial vision are repeated over and over. When Walt Disney died, the corporation drifted for years without the new vision and effective leadership of their current administration.

Vision and the ability to incorporate it into the culture require a dynamic and strong personality. Employees and management have to identify with the CEO Often these CEOs are good communicators and can make others understand where they want to go and how they are going to get there.

Stories are told in the Bean organization of how "L.L." would "charge around the store" when some product failed. It is evident that everyone knew what was on the CEO's mind. Joyce C. Hall of Hallmark was also adamant about quality. He is quoted as saying, "I'm hellbent on quality." Everyone knew his priorities. Until 1966 when he stepped aside as CEO so his son, Donald L. Hall, could take over, no greeting card reached the marketplace without his O.K.J.C. imprint.

It takes more than a clear focus to be able to impart a CEO's vision. It seems that most of these CEOs were truly liked or at least respected by their employees. It was a family atmosphere and in many cases, the CEO seems to have represented the benevolent father figure. Both Walton and Hall made conscious efforts to know as many of their people as possible. L.L. Bean and Stack considered employees as friends. There is mutual openness, trust, and respect.

If a culture is to be changed it appears to be much easier when the CEO is respected and admired. Leadership is given as much as it is taken. There is a decidedly human side to these CEOs that endears them to their employees. One store manager at Wal-Mart relayed the story of when he needed to be near a medical facility for one of his children. Walton arranged for him to be the manager of a store near a regional medical center. Such actions ensure that personnel adopt the CEO's vision more than a book full of policies, procedures, and regulations.

Similar stories in other top-level service organizations relay the CEO's humanitarian concerns. People in those organizations *know* the CEO cares; they know he is not a cold technocrat. Vision begins with a clear focus on what the organization represents and ends with human traits that create respect, admiration, and desire by personnel to carry out the CEO's desires.

PRINCIPLE 2
DEVELOP A STRATEGIC NICHE

Strategy is finding and developing the unique service or services that enable a business to "get a leg up" on the competition. It involves a business's particular service attributes and perspective, which the customer appreciates and will support with patronage.

It would be nice to provide 100% good service and 100% good products in all fields at all times, in every area, at minimum cost; but this obviously is not possible. Each business has to choose their strengths and provide services that accentuate those strengths and deemphasize their weaknesses. Many service providers even focus on particular types of customers. "Many new market entrants are adopting a market niche strategy, designing and positioning their services to appeal to specific market segments, rather than trying to be all things to all people" [1].

PRINCIPLE 3
TOP MANAGEMENT MUST DEMONSTRATE SUPPORT

It seems that no matter what the subject, one of the key issues is management commitment. It takes deeds and action to prove management's commitment to quality. As our service providers have shown, there are a variety of ways upper management can prove their support for quality.

One upper manager of a medical organization said, "My firm conviction is that you only get good quality (or anything else) by constant management insistence on it. There is no magic wand that you wave." He said it takes time, but it is time well spent. He remarked, "I say what I want and the next time they come up for salary review they had better be looking to improve service." He went on to say that it is not an adversarial situation. He said "Personnel know that if it is near and dear to my heart, when it comes time for evaluation I will use it to evaluate their performance." He emphasized that it is not really a matter of using a hammer; instead, it is mostly a matter of showing what service is costing the company. He makes a point of having the financial manager show everyone how much poor service is costing the company. He said, "You make a good story (financial facts) to begin with, then be absolutely open. Absolute candor is critical in dealing with people." This is a direct approach, but there are other ways for top management to show their support for quality service.

In our case involving American Airlines' incentive-based suggestion program, it was easy to see Chairman Crandall's support and commitment for that style of participatory management. Videotapes were made explaining its importance to the corporation. Training and an extensive and systematic use of incentives were employed, as well as the use of seminars and workshops.

For five years, Southwest Airlines has had the lowest customer complaint rate in the industry. Their president had a policy of constantly being involved at the ground level. He continuously asked for suggestions, gave recognition, and focused on teambuilding and promoting teamwork. He would even regularly unload baggage or otherwise pitch in as he fraternized with his people [2].

American Express' Jim Robinson frequently says the company's success depends on four factors: "quality, quality, quality, and quality." He is known as a zealot for quality. It has been reported that Mariott's CEO, Bill Mariott, constantly inspects the operational details, such as determining if bed linen is properly pressed or if the 66 steps in preparing a guest's room are being followed [1].

Sam Walton and his top-level managers constantly try to keep in touch with their store personnel. They have been known to ride with their truck drivers and always seem to be listening to their operational employees. This approach not only helps keep an operational perspective in upper management, but it also shows everyone in the company that management has a personal interest in the employee and a consumer perspective.

Personal visibility is not the only way management can show their commitment. American Express' quality personnel report directly to upper management. This is also the case for G.E.'s Answer Center, which handles G.E.'s customer complaints and inquiries. Its manager reports directly to a G.E. executive vice president. This system ensures that problems and opportunities are addressed. Hallmark's benefit program and Nissan's extensive wellness programs also demonstrate management support to employees. Wal-Mart's, SRC's and L.L. Bean's profit sharing and Employee Assistance Programs leave little doubt of management's priorities.

All of the effective service providers have earned the cooperation and loyalty of their front-line service providers. Their monetary, as well as nonmonetary, means of demonstrating this support varies, but the message is still the same: management cares and knows the value of their people in providing quality service.

PRINCIPLE 4
UNDERSTAND YOUR BUSINESS

This seems simple enough, doesn't it? If it is so simple and makes such sense, why isn't it more common? Most managers, as well as employees, seem to have a kind of tunnel vision. They understand their jobs, but they may never get the big picture, and that is risky for business and service.

Often, marketing only knows how to promote and advertise. Sales personnel can also be guilty of a limited focus. Many of them don't recognize that it's better to give customers a delivery date they are unhappy with, but that is feasible, than to give them an unrealistic date that the corporation is unlikely to meet. Sometimes salespeople misunderstand the fact that unless production can deliver on those promises, the entire organization suffers. Salespeople, like others, must understand their jobs and responsibilities within the context of the whole organization. The adage, "only promise what you can deliver and deliver what you promise" is sometimes misunderstood. Finance, accounting, and other "money types" look to positioning the corporation, and cash flow and investments, but often seem oblivious of the impact of their decisions on the ability of an organization to provide quality service.

This "hall of shame" list could go on and on. Most people know their specialty, but few know what it takes to deliver the goods and provide the services. Intimate understanding of this aspect of business is what the exceptional service providers have in common.

The means of developing this understanding among their personnel varies from one organization to another. The simplest way is to build this understanding from the ground up as Pepsi-Cola General Bottlers, Nordstrom, and Domino's do. They *promote their managers up through the ranks.* All of their managers started out in the lowest level operational job, usually as drivers, with Pepsi and Domino's. Whether it is delivering pizza, colas, or working on the sales floor, each individual, by the nature of the job, developed a basic understanding of what it takes to provide a quality product and service. A variation of this approach is used by Embassy Suites president Hervey Feldman's promotion of general managers who share his particular way of obtaining service. He places a lot of value on interpersonal skills and treating people as competent individuals.

These methods are simple but effective ways of building managerial understanding of what it takes to provide quality service and products, but may not always be feasible or even the most appropriate approaches. SRC and Pepsi-Cola General Bottlers, among others, have a process of *job rotation within management disciplines.* Many of these organizations' mid-level managers have worked in a variety of jobs despite being trained in other disciplines. Jack Stack, president of SRC, gives an example of this cross-fertilization of disciplines. He told of a records clerk who was moved to accounting. Later he was moved to material management and today he is director of marketing. Titles do not matter at SRC; everybody does the same thing: manage.

Although Pepsi-Cola General Bottlers' personnel do not interchange job titles as easily as those at SRC, they do have a detailed understanding of each other's duties. Marketing spends time every day in the production facilities and production spends time talking to marketing. There are frequent meetings and personal contact between these and other departments so that each has an intimate knowledge of each other. As Chip Peterson, the marketing manager noted, "Any one of us can do the other's job. We may not be as efficient at it, but we know what is involved in their job well enough that we can pitch in and do it if necessary."

In both of these cases, little attention is paid to job titles. The people involved know it is important to understand how each interacts with the other departments so they can react in a manner that is best for the whole organization. What is evident from these and other service providers is the fact that exposure to another's perspective is an extremely effective means of developing the "operational perspective" so critical to service success. It does take a great deal of effort and coordination to do this but, as the success of these organizations show, it is effort well worth the investment.

PRINCIPLE 5
APPLY OPERATIONAL FUNDAMENTALS

Southland Corporation, Tandy, Wal-Mart, and L.L. Bean all have exceptional service percentages. Those numbers did not happen by chance. All these organizations have exceptional distribution systems. Southland Corporation and Wal-Mart have even employed upper level managers who have worked in each other's systems. These two organizations and the others have several similarities. All of them also have efficient scheduling, organization, and basic "nuts and bolts" planning. In other words, they are operationally sound.

It is operations management that has led to their high levels of service. Service has nothing to do with promotions, advertising or marketing. Those might attract the customer's interest, but it's service, quality service, that keeps them, and it is operational management that provides the high level of service.

Operations or operational management is a branch of management emphasizing production techniques. This branch of management at one time was referred to as "scientific management," which was Fredrick Taylor's field. Later, as more and more techniques were applied to manufacturing, it became known as "production management." Even later it was changed to "operations management" as more and more services began adopting its techniques.

These operations or production techniques are the same regardless of whether they are being applied to manufacturing or services. The techniques consist of analytical methodologies and other models that come from disciplines as diverse as mathematics, statistics, and economics. Operations involves preparing forecasts, selecting processes and product designs, choosing a facility's location and layout, procuring materials, scheduling work, managing inventory and materials, maintaining equipment, and applying quality control techniques.

Every one of these service providers is grounded in strong operational fundamentals. SRC has good ratios between direct and indirect labor, controls overhead, and makes effective use of materials, equipment, and personnel. Southland, Wal-Mart, Tandy and others fill orders in an organized and efficient manner. Effective quality control, inspection, testing, and measurement are reasons these companies can be reliable and dependable. Managers grounded in the operational fundamentals, like those at American Express, Domino's, and Pepsi-Cola General Bottlers, are the ones who consistently deliver the service.

Good operations management is what good service is based on. For instance, "satisfaction guaranteed" is a powerful tool that quality service providers use to enhance their image and gain the customer's respect. Satisfaction guarantees cannot be a reality unless operations management can deliver the services. Those that offer the guarantee usually have 97% plus dependability and responsiveness. Anything less would be corporate suicide.

Successful service providers, even those primarily geared to sales and marketing, know the value of operations. Rasmussen [3] reports that American Express provides all of their general managers, most of whom come from sales or marketing, with a better appreciation of operations through seminars and written guides. These seminars aim to explain methodology and show "how various functions in operations link and interact with marketing, sales, and finance."

If a company wants to improve service by reducing turnaround time, then operational knowledge is imperative. If it is necessary, as is often the case, to combine department functions, better use capacity, streamline the process, or change a sequence of work to improve services then it will require operational expertise. The motivation may come from customers and management, but the means to improve comes from operations.

PRINCIPLE 6
UNDERSTAND, RESPECT, AND MONITOR THE CUSTOMER

Perhaps the best single way to develop an effective service strategy is to simply listen to your customers. Generally, customers are willing to tell business what they want, if only business would listen—really listen! Listening takes more than simply making complaint cards or forms available to customers, as many of the hotel chains do. Business needs to actively listen. They need to creatively seek ways of enhancing their awareness of all of their customer attitudes, preferences, and desires. Effective listening takes an aggressive attitude.

Understanding consumer desires requires continuous personal feedback checks. What we sometimes think or assume to be the customer's desires are often unrelated to what they really want. An executive told of one such case. It seems that he used to work for a company that tried to "build a better diaper." Research and development worked to develop the best diaper available. Finally, after years of work, they had perfected a diaper that could hold up to half a gallon of water. It was far superior to anything on the market. The trouble was that they missed the market. While others were selling a diaper of less reliability, they were perfecting their product. Much too late they discovered that the customer did not care if the diaper would hold one-half gallon of water because babies do not "release" that much before they are changed. They had good quality, or at least what they thought was good quality. Unfortunately they never asked the customer, they just *assumed* they knew. Today that company is out of the baby diaper business.

The lesson here is simple. Do not assume; instead make sure, as Southland Corporation, American Express and other service providers do, that your personal views mesh with those of your customers. Be aggressive about listening. Stop customers and ask them about the service. Talk to sales people. Find out what is and is not done well. Seek opinions and suggestions from all fronts. Find out what the competition is doing successfully. Ask customers how you stack up against the competition. It may be painful, but it is essential information.

Consumer feedback and satisfaction must be a primary goal of a corporation if service is to be improved. There should be a consumer perspective within the corporate culture. A consumer perspective can be developed within an organization by having everyone and every department think of each other as a customer. Solid State's use of internal measures of quality helped develop this perspective because each department more clearly saw how they were affecting other departments. In turn, they saw more clearly how their quality was being affected by other departments. Sales measures of consumer satisfaction, like delivery dates, were affected by production. The production control department's paper errors, in turn, affected sales accuracy in reporting delivery dates. Accounting's control of accounts receivable and cash flow affected the sales and production's ability to offer quality services and products. If the corporation does not have the money and credit rating, they cannot secure the best discounts, vendor contracts, etc.

Measuring these consumer indexes (non-conforming calls, paper errors, etc.) is a positive means of developing a consumer perspective, but there are other ways to strengthen this perspective. Usually departments that measure their customer performance, as Solid State does, will measure their outputs (e.g., cash flow, errors). Thus, the departments that deliver the services are the ones that create the measures. It would be far more effective if those departments would measure *outcomes* rather than outputs. Instead of setting up unrelated measures, have the department that consumes or receives the service do the measuring, reporting, and rating. When the department or individual that consumes your services does the evaluation, it becomes more realistic and relevant.

Production would rate the service they get from personnel or sales. Accounting, computing, and so forth would measure, report, and rate those services they receive. This way those that must consume poor or good quality from those "upstream" could have greater influence. All organizational departments and individuals are interdependent. Setting up such an outcome program would certainly make everyone more aware and more effective in delivering services that *are* needed, not what they thought was needed. It could significantly reduce tunnel vision and enhance qualitivity.

Report cards are an important means of improving services. All of these top-notch service providers have some means of reporting on the level of their service. As already noted, Holiday Inn invests $1 million a year just to monitor the customer. Other ways of reporting service include Domino's mystery customer program and Southland Corporation's emphasis on executives spending time in their stores. L.L. Bean has a unique way to report on the quality of their service. Their own managers test products and act as customers. Obviously, there is a variety of means of getting customer feedback. The important point is to do a service audit in as systematic a way as possible.

PRINCIPLE 7
USE APPROPRIATE TECHNOLOGY

Technology by itself is neither good nor bad. In service it is how it is used that determines whether it is appropriate or not. Consider the use of computers to monitor the performance of operations. In some cases, as at Texas Instrument's CRC, technology is used in a positive way. Managers at top quality service providers use technology in a positive way to *enhance* quality service. They use technology that automatically routes phone calls to available operators. They monitor calls and responses, but rely more on peer pressure and professional pride to help control operators.

Contrast this CRC approach to the "sweat shop" environment of some of the 800-number centers and many reservation systems. They focus on production with little thought to the quality of the interaction. The number of interactions rather than the quality of the interaction is what is important.

Speed or efficiency without quality is not effectiveness. Computers in sweat shop environments are used to monitor the telephone operators' calls and to measure their performance. The focus here is decidedly different than at CRC and so is the outcome. If a difficult problem arises with customers and they are taking up too much time, it can destroy the performance rating of the telephone operator. Operators have been known to fake a disconnection when the customer's questions are complex or will take too much time to answer. This assembly-line mentality is great for short-term improvements in productivity, but long-term quality and image are severely damaged through such tactics. This is an inappropriate use of technology typical of services and manufacturers that are "flying by the seat of their pants."

Quality service providers make appropriate use of technology because they have a plan. Southland Corporation's use of the ESP technology that helps place merchandise on store shelves so roominess, profits, and turnover can be improved is appropriate technology. This, along with flatbed scanners and the possible use of satellites to help in communications with delivery trucks, is appropriate technology because it places them *closer to their customers.*

L.L. Bean also recognizes the proper place of technology. As noted earlier, Thomas C. Day said he preferred to use computers more in planning and control. He said he liked to use them more to direct the manual effort and less for machinery needs. L.L. Bean's customer service computers and automatic equipment helps process customer questions. Their use of technology is not to replace people, but to *enhance service.*

Technology can be an important means of improving services, provided its use fits within the goals of improving services and becoming closer to the customer. Poor service providers seem to think of their people as a necessary evil or at least as ineffective. They would like to use the technology to eliminate employees or to reduce their impact on the organization. On the other hand, quality service providers recognize that while technology might be important, it is their people who are critical to quality service. These companies recognize technology as nothing but a tool to help their people do a better job.

PRINCIPLE 8
THE NEED TO INNOVATE

Service providers must continually explore new ways of providing services to their customers. This does not mean that it is necessary to be on the "cutting edge." Not everyone can or should be on the cutting edge of their respective industries, but every business should explore opportunities. What is required is management attention focused on fundamental questions about their services. They should examine who, what, where, when, and how services are delivered. They should ask: is it (service) enough? Is there a better way? Are they delivering what the customer wants or just what is expected?

Future-oriented service providers seek ways of turning research and development (R&D) to a competitive advantage. These successful businesses continuously search for new products and services that can help them differentiate themselves in today's competitive market. The Office of Technology Assessment has suggested that firms producing services pay for about a quarter of all U.S. industrial R&D [4].

It is clear that technology and/or innovation can, under the right conditions, improve both services and corporate competitiveness. As already shown, Domino's, Southland Corporation, American Express, and Holiday

Inn all improved their competitiveness through a variety of innovations. For instance, American Airlines improved their competitiveness by introduction of their Sabre Reservation system. Such state-of-the-art technology that makes it quicker and easier to book customers is an enormous advantage. Other customer service innovations include introduction of discount fares in 1948 for families flying together; super-saver programs in 1977; and the AAdvantage program in 1981 that rewarded frequent flyers. All these industry innovations certainly improved their competitiveness. Similar innovations, as well as employee involvement innovations, enhance both the service and profitability of service companies.

The Office of Technology Assessment has noted, "Technology . . . viewed as encompassing skills, expertise, know-how and work organization . . . is a major competitive weapon" even in many services such as tourism, shipping, fast foods, retail trade, banking, insurance and health care [4]. For example, they noted that fast food restaurants must define menu, manage high turnover workforce with limited skills and expenses, cope with output that varies greatly, and so forth. They have to decide how to organize production to give customers what they want, where they want it, and at a minimum cost. They have to constantly innovate or their competition will innovate them right out of business.

Perhaps noting a future trend, the Office of Technology Assessment said, "Service firms have begun to create what are, in effect, R&D arms, even if they do not think of them as such." They further noted that the United States is not evolving toward a service economy; rather it is evolving toward a high-skill economy . . . one where R&D and new applications of technology play an even greater role [4]. Service companies are increasingly looking to innovations as a way to create new or enhance old services and products, establish new markets and customers, and provide better customer service.

PRINCIPLE 9
HIRE THE RIGHT PEOPLE

Customers want to be treated with common courtesy. They want someone who will help, who can and wants to handle problems. Some of these traits can be developed through training, but a lot depends on finding the right people for a particular business. This is becoming a major challenge. With the coming labor shortage it will be difficult enough to find any new employees, not to mention finding ones that match a business's unique needs. It will be the well-run companies, the ones who respect their employees and customers, that will be successful.

Greater employee accountability, responsibility, and authority will be necessary attributes of companies that want to attract the best (employees).

Companies like Wal-Mart, American Express, Federal Express, and SRC do not have so much trouble finding applicants. SRC is able to find the right people for them because they have a reputation as a good employer. They've had over 3,000 applicants for 300 positions at their main facility. Incidentally, this occurs despite the fact that their base wage ranges from $6.00 to $7.00 an hour in an area where $10.00 an hour wages are paid for the same type of employee.

The positive impact of a good reputation is not limited to SRC. Marion Laboratories, a respected and nationally known employer located in Kansas City, has similar good fortune. In 1986, they had 12,000 applications for 125 sales positions. Of course, reputation alone is not enough to ensure hiring the right people.

At SRC, no employee, past or present, has been hired based on only one opinion. Prospective employees will be interviewed by two to five managers of areas where the employee might work. SRC's Human Resources Department is responsible for recruiting and screening prospective employees who might "fit in," but each prospective employee has to talk to several managers before being hired. After the series of interviews, managers discuss the prospective employee and if any one of this group expresses a negative impression, the applicant is dropped from consideration.

SRC uses the normal recruiting agencies (state employment office, professional recruiters) but they ask these agencies to tour the facilities and learn what type of work is involved with each job. Despite SRC's willingness to accept applicants from many sources, the greatest number of prospective employees are referred by current employees. Human Resources Director Gary Brown says, "Fully 70% of the people we hire come from employee referrals."

When an employee suggests someone for a position, he or she is asked to submit a *recommendation to hire* form. Brown emphasizes that in doing so, the employee places reputation and credibility on the line. Brown said everyone is aware of this and they will not submit someone's name for consideration unless they feel very sure the person will be a good employee.

SRC comprehensively checks the employee's professional and personal references. Even if a prospective employee has only worked part-time in the summer, hauling hay, SRC will contact that employer, and any teacher, pastor, or other person who can shed light on the applicant's work ethic and attitudes.

G.E.'s Answer Center, which handles customer information, complaints, and requests, has even gone so far as to identify personality traits and abilities critical to the development of telephone agents. They then reinforce these attributes with five weeks of initial training. Reinforcement continues with another 100 hours of training annually. Whatever the traits and methods of enhancing those characteristics, the message is clear. If you want good service, you have to find good people to deliver it.

PRINCIPLE 10
PROVIDE SKILL-BASED TRAINING

James D. Robinson, American Express' CEO has noted, "We have a two-part pledge to customers: first, to promise only what we can deliver; second, to deliver what we promise. And we deliver our service one transaction at a time. It is our well-trained employees who make this technology work— who ultimately deliver what we promise" [5].

Skill-based training is more than learning good manners, politeness, or to "smile and dial." Skill-based training focuses on developing ways to improve quality service. The training should not be approached in a piecemeal manner. Training should be designed to teach employees and managers the basic skills needed to improve services.

Even seasonal workers (traditionally an undependable group in terms of turnover, absenteeism, and motivation) can be taught to be effective service providers with the right training. L.L. Bean handles six million packages a year and has a turnaround time of four and one-half days. Their 99%-plus accuracy rate is accomplished largely by part-time or seasonal workers. At L.L. Bean, even seasonal workers get one week of introductory training. Walt Disney World has the same strong belief in extensive training even for very low-skilled service jobs.

The length of the training or its formal structure is not necessarily related to its effectiveness. Nordstrom only has a day and a half of training. Even poor service providers have some training. It is the *substance*, not the style, that is important.

American Airlines, SRC, and other top service providers use different approaches, but the results are the same. They have a committed and concerned workforce that gives extra effort; their training is built on respect for the intelligence of their personnel.

PRINCIPLE 11
SET STANDARDS, MEASURE PERFORMANCE, AND ACT

Instituting a customer perspective is easier when goals are set, performance is measured, and then compared to the standards. If there is a deviation between what is expected (standards) and what is achieved (actual behavior), then there is room for improvement. Many improvements in services cannot occur unless it is possible to find out what is currently being done.

Perhaps the single biggest way to improve services is to set service goals, but this realistically cannot occur unless we find some way to measure performance. Once performance is measured it is possible to motivate and then reward those that go beyond minimum standards. And then it is much easier to instill a corporate service culture because hiring, employment, and promotion decisions can be based on quality service standards.

Front-line personnel and their managers must understand that they are expected to improve. Most will improve once they know the rules. As the phrase goes, "I can play any game—just teach me the rules." Standards are the rules and monitoring them provides competent people with a means of gaining control. As one manager noted about the recent installation of service performance measures, "I always knew our department contributed to the success of the company; now everyone knows, including my boss."

Like technology, standard setting and measurement can be powerful tools, but only if they are properly used. In the wrong hands or with the wrong objective they can actually lead to poor performance and poor quality. The 800-number sweat-shop telephone centers are examples of poor use of standards. If merit and incentives are based on performance to standards, then it is essential that those standards be reasonable, achievable, relevant, clearly communicated, and focused on qualitivity.

When American Express implemented their standards they made a point of first getting employees to understand the specific standards they had set for service. Next, they let employees know what was expected of each one and how individual performance would be measured against the standards. They emphasized that this process would be an important part of an employee performance appraisal. They also made a point of showing employees the cost of poor quality. Finally, they rewarded quality service performance.

PRINCIPLE 12
ESTABLISH INCENTIVES

When we motivate people and give them the authority necessary, almost anything is possible. Our top level service providers found a variety of ways to positively motivate performance. For instance, the store sales personnel at Nordstrom are given a basic wage and then receive a commission on everything they sell to customers. Unlike many service personnel they have a direct connection between effort and results. Store sales personnel work to build a group of clients since they get a commission on everything they sell.

Profit sharing, pay, and benefit packages also offer incentives for work even though the reinforcement is not as immediate or direct. The important point is to remember that people must see the connection between action and results. People are intelligent and they expect to be paid in some way for their service results.

Regardless of the monetary or nonmonetary incentives used to improve service, two things are needed to make the effective organization and commitment. Top management must create and actively support an effective incentive program. This means devoting sufficient money, time, and effort to ensure that front-line service personnel treat it seriously.

Desire is always important, but effort must be well-organized if it is to be effective. For instance, a wide variety of incentives must be available to appeal to employees' individual needs and desires. Incentives should not only be extensive, but systematic as well. Incentives are only as strong as the weakest link. If a supervisor or middle manager or someone who must implement the idea, process or project is not encouraged to change his or her behavior, little system-wide change will occur. Incentives and rewards to improve services must be aimed at everyone up through the organization so everyone has a stake in improving service. It is the intelligent and profitable thing to do.

KEY POINTS

The goal of these twelve principles is to help management improve service, thereby creating customer loyalty and profitability. These twelve principles can be distilled down to three key concepts.

The first is the need for *management action.* Management must have a clear vision of what they want, focus everyone's efforts on that vision, and be respected by the personnel within the organization who must implement the vision. Having chosen a specific service strategy management thinks will be successful, they must then be willing to prove their support for the service strategy.

All too often, management does a lot of talking, issues directives and memos, but changes little. For instance, top management often talks about participation and the need to "communicate" then turns around and makes all the important decisions and fails to solicit the advice of subordinates. Such action sends mixed signals and does more harm than those managers who never made false promises in the first place. For quality service to exist, top management must become directly involved. They must demonstrate their commitment through deeds, personal involvement in the service programs, and maintaining close contact with those responsible for implementing quality service.

The second key concept is the need to approach service in a *systematic manner.* The best intentions will not produce results until programs are in place that are able to convert ideas into actions. Systems must be set up so people, managers as well as employees, understand how and why a business runs as it does and what is needed from everyone to provide the service necessary to ensure customer loyalty and profits. Systems must be set up to make sure the right tools and technology are installed so they mesh with people to produce an effective, not merely efficient, service. Systems must be set up so the organization is constantly examining new ways and new approaches to service and how it is delivered.

Systems must be set up so customers do not get lost in the process. Customers will tell you what they want and do not want. They will tell management what is acceptable to them, but it is extremely easy to lose contact with them. Most importantly, every effort needs to be made to actively solicit input from *all* of an organization's customers.

Finally, the last concept for good service is *people.* People can overcome a great many flaws in the other two concepts. Service lives and dies on the individual transactions of each front-line and support employee. Great effort needs to be put into finding the right people for each of these key positions. Once having found them, management cannot afford to ignore them. Unfortunately, often management does seem to spend more effort recruiting people rather than retaining them. Top service providers spend great effort training and motivating their personnel. They know good service depends on them. If personnel are treated fairly, respected, and given positive attention, they are much more likely to treat the customer the same way.

REFERENCES

1. Lovelock, Christopher H., "Developing and Managing the Customer-Service Function in the Service Sector," in *The Service Encounter: Managing Employee/Customer Interaction,* John A. Czepiel, Michael R. Soloman, and Carol F. Suprenant (eds.), Lexington, Massachusetts, D.C. Heath and Company, 1985, p. 269.
2. Rieder, George A., "Show M. The Secret to Building a Service-Minded Culture," *Zale Retailing Letter,* Vol. II, No. 2, June, 1986.
3. Rasmussen, MaryAnne E., "Ensuring Quality on a Worldwide Basis," *American Productivity Center Quality Forum,* July 14, 1987, p. 9.
4. Alic, J. A., "R&D in the Services," Paper presented at the Annual Meeting of the American Association for the Advancement of Science, Boston, Mass., February 11–15, 1988.
5. "The Quality Imperative," (Paid Advertising Section), *Fortune,* Sept. 29, 1986.

Index

American Express, 17–20, 23–29, 33–36
Artificial intelligence, 36, 66–67
Assessment tools, 73–80
Autonomy, 128–131
Awards, 54, 121–123

Better service, 6–9
Bureaucracy, 12, 62
Byerlys', 61–69, 128

CEO vision, 139–141
Climate surveys, 135
Commodity budgets, 18–19
Communication, 134–137
Complaint-handling, 1
Conventional service, 62–65
Cost focus, 63
Courtesy, 104–105
Customer expectations, 84–85
Customer relations, 16
Customer surveys, 71–73
    transaction-based, 91
Customers
    assessing, 30–32, 71–80
    complaints, 1–3
    expectations, 2–3, 73–74
    feedback, 46, 147–148
    perspective, 32, 51–53, 146–148
    report cards, 7, 148
    research, 33–35
    service, 61
    staying close, 30–32

Dead-on-arrival (D.O.A.), 22
Decentralized management, 126–137
Dedication, 25–26
Defining customer expectations, 73–74
Defining service, 83–85
Delegation, 11, 128–135
Demographics, 28–29
Dependability, 39–47
Dissatisfied customers, 1–2, 4–5
Distribution systems, 45
Domino's Pizza, 49–59

ESP, 140
Efficient shelf planning (ESP), 33, 35–36
Employee
    attitude, 103–106
    communication, 17–19
    dedication, 25–26
    feedback, 43, 113, 134–136
    involvement, 24, 133–134
    loyalty, 43
    motivation, 17
    orientation, 101–102
    selection, 101–102
    suggestions, 109–119
    training, 17–19, 97–101
Entrepreneurial management, 128–137
Expert systems, 36

Federal Express, 10, 50–52, 54
Front line service providers, 5

Guarantees, 40–41

High technology, 35–37, 52
Hiring, 150–151

Incentives, 26, 108–125, 153–154
  individual, 122
  monetary, 119–121
  profit sharing, 120–121
  recognition, 121, 123
  systematic, 54, 111–119
Innovation, 149–150
Innovative strategy, 67
Involvement circles, 127–128
Involving employees, 24, 133–134

Job rotation, 144
Job standards, 19–23

Leading-by-example, 24
L.L. Bean, 39–40
Loyal employees, 25–26

Management
  bureaucratic, 17, 62
  commitment, 20, 142–143
  support groups, 23, 25
  vision, 139–141
Management-by-exception, 93
Managerial job rotation, 144
Managerial recognition, 121–123
Market niche, 60–69, 141–142
Market research, 28–29, 33–35
Measuring performance, 152–153
Meetings, 135
Monitoring customers, 15–17,
  146–148
Motivation
  employee, 17–19
Mystery customer program, 51–52

Nonconforming
  calls, 76–77
  costs, 74–75
Nontraditional employee training,
  97–101
Nordstrom, 11

On-the-job training, 18–19
Open communication, 134–137
Operational management, 44–45,
  145–146

Participative management, 126–137
Peak performance through
  commitment, 133
Peer pressure, 10–11
Perceived risk, 65
Performance
  and commitment, 133
Performance standards, 19–23,
  53–55, 83–84, 100, 152–153
Principles of service, 139–155
Production management, 44–45,
  145–146
Productivity, 9–12
Profit sharing, 120–121
Promotion from within, 144
Proprietary programs, 66–67

Qualitivity, 9–11
Quality circles, 127–128
Quality of worklife (QWL),
  131–133
Quality standards, 19–23, 83–84,
  100, 152–153
Quality testing, 19–23, 40–42

Recruitment, 150–151
Reliability, 39–47
Report cards, 7, 148
Research and development,
  149–150
Responsible autonomy, 128–131

Responsible service, 49–59
Responsiveness, 48–49, 52–53, 59
Reward menu, 118
Rewarding good behavior, 133
Rewards, 54, 100–125, 153–154
    monetary, 119–121
    recognition, 121–123

Sales service measures, 76–77
Satisfaction guaranteed, 40–41
Self-assessment surveys, 73–74
Sensitivity to customers, 71–72
Service
    incentives, 108–125
    inferior, 4–6
    perspectives, 65–68
    standards, 19–23, 53–55, 83–84,
        100, 152, 153
    suggestion programs, 108–119
    systematic approach, 154
    training, 96–107
Service-minded personnel, 25–26
Service-oriented, 32–33
Service simplicity, 55–56
Service and speed, 48–59
Service Tracking Report (STR), 73
Simplicity, 55–57
Social technology, 43
Southland Corporation, 16, 19–37
Specialization, 55–57
Standards
    establishing, 89–91
    of performance, 19–23, 53–55,
        83–84, 100, 152–153

Strategy, 67, 141–142
Stress management, 103
Suggestion teams, 132
Support groups, 23–25
Surveys, 71–73, 91
Systematic incentives, 54

Technical Assistance Research
    Programs (TARP), 1, 7
Technology, 35–37, 42–46, 148–149
Testing for quality, 19–23, 40, 42
Texas Instruments, 10–11, 15–17,
    25–26
Thoughtfulness, 104–105
Training, 96–107, 152
    employee, 17–19
    on-the-job, 18–19
    skill-based, 152
Trusting employees, 18
Turnaround time, 76

Unconditional guarantees, 40–41
Understanding customers, 24–25,
    146–147
Understanding your business, 49–50
Unhappy customers, 1–2, 4–5

Vision, 139–141

Wal-Mart, 16, 18, 21, 45
Wellness programs, 120